BL

DAVID DANIELS III

BLACK & BLUE *In Bridgeport*
Copyright © 1995 - 2023 David Daniels, III
Published By: David Daniels III / F. Alexander
ISBN: 979-8-223-8020B-2
Edited & Cover Art By: F. Alexander
All rights reserved. Without limiting the rights under copyright reserved above, no part of this publication may be reproduced, stored in or introduced into a retrieval system, or transmitted, in any form, or by any means (electronic, mechanical, photocopying, recording, or otherwise) without the prior written permission of both the copyright owner and the above author of this book. Names, characters, places, brands, media, and some incidents are used fictitiously. The author acknowledges the trademarked status and trademark owners of various products or businesses are referenced in this work, which have been used without permission.

Table of Contents

DEDICATION 1
PROLOGUE 4
Chapter I | The Authorities | Make No Statements 7
Chapter II | One Major Step | Number 616 14
Chapter III | The Prospect | Inception 26
Chapter IV | Becoming Blue | Hidden Costs 41
Chapter V | The Ups, Downs and Joy | Stormy Weather 56
Chapter VI | Year of the Rookie | How The Game Is Played 63
Chapter VII | Uncivilized Brutality | You See and Don't See 68
Chapter VIII | The Seventies | Growing Up 94
Chapter IX | Officer Lawbreaker | Meat or Grass Eater 108
Chapter X | White Before Blue | Internal Infestation 112
Chapter XI | Fighting Back | Banding Together 124
Chapter XII | Needing A Boost | After Your Shift 141
Chapter XIII | Each One, Help One | Back Stabbing 145
Chapter XIV | Who's The Leader | A New Day 157
Chapter XV | Farewell Tour | Next Episode 171
ABOUT THE AUTHOR 184

DEDICATION

My Parents:
David Daniels, Jr. - In loving memory
Jean Carolyn Daniels - To the best mother any man could ever have.
You mean the world to me
To MY hood - P.T. Barnum Housing Projects
To MY City – The Park City, Bridgeport, Connecticut
My Mentors:
Ted Meekins, Alexander Norwood and Ernest L. Parker
Thank you for a lifetime of guidance in the right direction
NABLEO, NBPA & NOBLE
Thanks for being a big part of my career
My fellow Officers Countrywide that have transitioned to their End of Watch
We remember you
Those Whom Left Too Early:
Willie Bowman, Sarah J. Crockett, Taylor M. Daniels, William R. Daniels, Janine C. Daniels and Steve Smalls
May you all rest in peace and have my eternal love
My Family and Family of Friends
Thank you for your love and support of me and my endeavors over the course of my many years
My Children:

DAVID DANIELS, III

Joy C. Daniels, Marvin Tyson, David Daniels IV, Deja Y. Daniels and Gene I. Daniels

I wanted to be the one to tell you my story, my unconditionally loved.

The Lord's Many Blessings
Thank you Lord for allowing me to take it this far

BLACK & BLUE IN BRIDGEPORT

PROLOGUE

During the twenty-five years and seven months that was my career as a Bridgeport, Connecticut Police Officer, I saw many people come and then go. With the job being so demanding, the pressures were constant and so many did not and could not make it for the long run. Those that disappeared did so for various reasons. Some left the job early, others were forced out and sadly some died along the way. Then, there is the group that I fell into. We are labeled the lucky ones. The lucky ones persevered. They pressed on and lasted long enough to retire and collect their pension. I agree and do consider myself one of the lucky ones.

I have had the unique opportunity to travel quite a bit in my career field. I met, talked with and learned from other police officers from all over this country. I've learned about them, the places they police and mostly about their departments. From all my interactions, I came to realize that Bridgeport's Police Department is just a microcosm of other police departments across the country. I had once believed that our internal problems with policing were just ours. Sad to say, but most departments are no different when it comes to being racially polarizing and non-functional. So, Bridgeport Police Department's problems are not unique, but the implications of these practices continuing in the future, is scary. In a nut shell, the police are too busy fighting one another to have any real or lasting effects on crime in their communities.

BLACK & BLUE IN BRIDGEPORT

During my time spent in the department, I've witnessed officers suffering mental illnesses, battling alcoholism and continuing to suffer with high divorce rates, which still plague our career field. In this profession, people are walking around like little powder kegs on the verge of blowing, while carrying guns on their sides. The department perpetually suffers with leadership crises that include being under the direction of leaders with checkered pasts and that breeds a lack of respect for the person in charge of running things. At one point, there were rumors that one of our highest ranking members was a serial killer.

I realized that this job, with all that officers have to endure, stripped me of some of my humanity. As a result, when my on-the-job tormentors experienced tragedies, injuries, family crises and death, I found myself unable to muster any compassion or pathos for them. At one point, I gave into feeling somewhat glad that they too had to experience some pain, since they were so good at dishing it out. Ultimately, I hope to regain that lost humanity someday. Some of the things I saw, the treachery and deceit, in this corrupt system will confound me for a lifetime. But thankfully, I lived through it all to be able to tell my story about the journey.

A journey where I had the best witness seat on the ride to experience the rise and fall of The Bridgeport Guardians, The National Black Police Association and a political takeover of The Bridgeport Police Department with its negative effects, police brutality, unwavering racism, poor city governmental leadership, diabolical corruption and much more. I saw people at their best and their worst. Through all the highs and lows and I will take you there, so you can see how I played the hand I was dealt. Traveling this road, I met some people I would not want to come across in a dark alley, but then there were also those that were the greatest human beings in the world. Looking back, I know that I was blessed. Blessed to walk away alive from the good, the bad and the ugly and a lifetime of unforgettable memories that will forever be my life and times.

DAVID DANIELS, III

Chapter I
The Authorities Make No Statements

As the Captain's eyes opened wide, his face went beet red and it seems like sweat instantly starts forming on his balding head. I can feel the heat building up, so I lean forward and tell him all the details of the incident from beginning to end. Once I pause, he immediately picks up the phone on his desk and begins to dial a number he seems familiar with. Sitting there just listening to him on the phone, made my heart sink. Sitting there hearing him repeat, word for word everything I had just said to him to someone else listening on the other end of the line. When he completes his call, he looks across at me and that's when things got even crazier.

"We are going to Internal Affairs and you will have to give them a statement."

Without a thought, I knew I did not want anything else like this to happen which could only make the situation worse.

"I don't want to go anywhere or give any statements, Captain!"

"I'm not asking you. I'm ordering you to do it, it's your job."

All I could do was sit there. I was totally numb inside while thinking back to when I dreamed of becoming a police officer and how I could have never imagined being in this position. Already dealing with all the accidents and my crumbling marriage, I had to now add this to the top of pile. If I didn't know before, I knew now. My life was getting ready to change, yet again for the worse, but this time it would be forever.

I don't even remember how I got to the Office of Internal Affairs, but their building was off-site and across town from the police department. Things were all happening so fast and all I knew was I had no power to stop any of it. Inside the building, I signed the visitors log then was lead into a small office. I gave my statement, it was recorded and then I was shown photos of the whole police force. It was made clear that they wanted a detailed account of what happened, who was there and what was said. In short, they wanted everything and this is why I told the Captain that I didn't want to make any statements. Telling the Captain everything was easy for me because it was the right thing to do. My thoughts were that he would keep it within the department, handle the situation and things would work themselves out. But now, it was outside the department and it was all on me to do the right thing again. So I did just that. I had no other choice, but to lie and I was not going to give into lying. I told them everything I remembered. I stated what happened, named names and recalled what was said. My testimony implicated three veteran Officers involved in the incident and it seemed like I was there for hours.

By now, the police department was in a buzz. While I was still at the Internal Affairs building, other officers were being called in to give their statements. It seemed like people were moving around everywhere, coming in and out. I was then taken to another office, off the beaten path, as to hide me from the officers coming in. Each officer had to sign the same log book that I signed when I came in so hiding me really did not matter. Plus, a Sergeant from headquarters made it a point to bring each officer right by the office I was now sitting in.

When I finally got home, I was emotionally drained, bewildered and depressed. I did not know who to turn to or who I could trust. I had been told by internal affairs not to discuss the situation with anyone. It seemed as if my whole world was unraveling like a ball of string or falling apart like a house of cards. That night in my solitude, I felt like a lost child who needed to be held. I tried to fight it by reminding myself that I was grown now. Still, I just needed someone, anyone just to tell me that things were going to be okay, but there was no one. Separated from my wife and daughter, I was alone. At one point, I even thought my wife may just like finding out that all of this was happening because we were still arguing back and forth and I thought she hated me. It was a sleepless night.

The next day, I went to visit my daughter and my wife happens to be there. I wanted to tell her that I am in trouble, so I tried to find the words. At some point during the visit, she looks at me and gives me the opportunity that I needed.

"I heard you're having some problems on the job?"

This is my chance, I thought. I can tell her right now and stop being alone with all this mess. I tell myself to go ahead, tell her everything. Instead, like a brick hitting me in the face, my fear jumps all over me. Fearing that she would enjoy hearing about my pain, on this job she never wanted me to take, forced me to just brush off her question.

"You should know me better than that."

My response, along with an assured expression on my face, ended her concern. Instantly, I felt horrible for not talking about it. I just stayed a little while longer, then left to go to work.

When I arrived at police headquarters, expecting to work my regular shift, I was quickly advised that I had been placed on suspension. This suspension was based on pending charges against me. I could not convey with any words what that felt like. I was then taken to Internal Affairs, yet again because they wanted more details. Once there, there were more pictures, more taped recordings and more questions like that which I had experienced the night before. The Internal Affairs Detective told me that I was suspended, along with the others so I would not be the object of attention, go figure. Back at

DAVID DANIELS, III

headquarters, I was told I still had to come to work every day only to be temporarily assigned to the front desk.

The next day, a story covering the incident hit the newspapers, clearly naming me and the others as being suspended. I could feel the tension and stares from my co-workers as I made my way through the building on my way to the front desk. People and Officers alike, were turning their backs to me and not speaking to me at all. At shift's end, I left work in my brand new Chevy Camaro with its windshield covered in spit.

In the coming weeks more spit and turned backs, followed by the dents and scratches that were showing up on my car. I was a bundle of raw nerves. It was hard just coming to work now. Dealing with everyone acting out like they were and worrying about protecting things like my car while trying to work. I started parking on the street instead of inside the parking lot, but that did no good.

I was finally taken off suspension, only to then be put on administrative notice. This meant that I had to face charges regarding the incident. From there, I was allowed to resume patrol duties, but I quickly found out that no officer would ride with me or back me up on calls. When I would return to headquarters at shift's end and attempt to turn in my paperwork, this particular Sergeant would scrutinize my paperwork. He would make me correct everything to his satisfaction, on the spot before he would give me the keys to the police garage to retrieve my car. Normal practice was to just turn in our paperwork and it would be handed back to you the next day, if anything needed correcting. I hated what that Sergeant was doing to me, but I rolled with it by paying more attention to my paperwork. When I was dispatched, that same Sergeant would get to the location before me and then leave without saying one word to me. The other Sergeants followed suit, really riding me hard and calling me out on everything little thing that they could. Again, it was tough, but it all was making me a better officer even though I know that was not their intent.

BLACK & BLUE IN BRIDGEPORT

During this time I was a pawn for transfers and had been transferred to at least three different squads. I would arrive at work only to be told that I had been transferred again. During one stretch I was off for eleven days straight due to all the transferring. If my voice was recognized on the police radio, my broadcasts were jammed so I couldn't get through to base. I received no back up on calls. I had to accept that if I found myself in a dangerous situation, I was on my own. No officer, in the whole department would back me up and I was driving a solo car without a partner.

After a few weeks of all this messy stuff going on, the Captain called me into his office and suggested I get a partner. I was transferred again. This time it was to the red sector of the city on Bridgeport's East End and my new partner was Officer Jerry Platt. Our area post started at the beginning of Stratford Avenue, down to the Stratford city line and continued up toward the Bridgeport Hospital area. This section of town, mostly consisting of minority citizens was also densely populated. This made for a high number of calls for service during our shifts. We encountered enhanced criminal activities from; gangs, drug dealing, bars, cleaners, neighborhood stores, several churches and even schools. It was a hot-bed of activity 24-7.

I had met Jerry in the police academy. He was southern, a little older than me and his wife was a veteran Officer. At first, we didn't hit it off too good. He was too gung-ho for me. I was just the opposite, just trying to stay low key. After all that I had been through, the one thing that I knew I was not is gung-ho, not at all. After the first week, Jerry did not want to ride with me anymore. We had a long talk and decided to give things another try. By this time the incident had become daily newspaper coverage. Everyone inside and outside the department was talking about it. How I was being treated was now taking a toll on Jerry and our partnership. Jerry helped me side-step some of the things the Sergeants were trying to pull on me. He told me that he did not agree with the way I was being treated.

DAVID DANIELS, III

By the third week of us riding together, a Connecticut Post Reporter wanted to ride with us and interview me about all the harassment stories that were beginning to emerge. He signed a waiver and was given the back seat of our police car for the tour. At first, I was reluctant to do the interview. I just wanted it all to go away. After hearing that the Sergeant, whom had been riding me for weeks, was against me doing the interview, I quickly changed my tune and agreed to do it. Jon Heller was the reporter. As he rode with us interviewing me, he saw the people in the community coming up to the police car to shake my hand and encourage me as we traveled the east end. Jon and I talked about everything that I had experienced. When he turned and asked Jerry how he felt about what was happening to me Jerry quickly replied with 'no comment.' Previously and in private, Jerry had expressed his opinion and understood why I had to do what I did. I expected him to speak up to the reporter, but he let me down. That made me a bit sad and I felt alone again. The Mayor, Police Chief and other working supervisors were supposed to be monitoring my radio calls during the interview. We were to receive only non-threatening calls during that period. Other cars in the sector were expected to give us cover, if there were any dangerous calls.

My last night on the streets, Jerry and I were sent to three 'shots fired' calls back to back. The last one took us to a bodega near East Main Street. There we discovered a young Hispanic male that had been shot and now lying in a pool of blood in the rear of the store. Someone in the store said that the shooter had just left and was running up the street. Jerry instantly jumped in the car, pulled off in search of the shooter and left me alone in the store with the victim. A crowd started to form. I tried to utilize the radio to convey my condition, but my transmissions were being blocked by other officers. Someone called for an ambulance by telephone and as it arrived, so did a Captain and a Lieutenant. They were my cover on this call, because no other car from that sector came to that location during the incident. After my shift, I finally got a chance to speak to Ted Meekins of the Guardians. After much discussion, I decided to request a transfer off the street. The very next night, the Police Commissioners granted my request to placed somewhere in the department where I could work with children.

Remembering growing up and how the adults around me only had bad things to say about police officers did not help me to become an officer. Knowing what I have come to learn about how officers can be, from the inside out, sheds some light on why departments fail their communities so much. I thought I was joining a new family. A bonded family, dedicated to protecting, serving and improving the lives of the city's citizens, but I was wrong. I would have never believed that fellow officers would turn their backs on me, while so many citizens rallied in support of my efforts. But from the beginning, it wasn't the police department or even the police force that created a desire in me to join. It was just one officer. One officer doing the right thing, at the right time for the people he served sparked my dream.

Chapter II
One Major Step
Number 616

Although January 6, 1986 could have ended as a typical cold winter's night in Connecticut, one thing 'never-wished-for' was about to change all that. Around 11:30 p.m., my sleep is interrupted by the telephone's ring. The caller is my youngest sister Ninky. Her call is to let me know that my younger brother Jeffrey had been shot and was being transported to Bridgeport Hospital. I slam down the phone, get dressed as fast as I can and raced off to the hospital.

Being met at the hospital by my sisters, they quickly tell me that Jeff is okay and that he's being prepped for surgery. As we continue talking, they begin telling me how Jeff wound up in this situation. Similar to other calls the police often get of domestic situations, my brother came home early, found someone in his home and that person shot him. The whole situation was bad, but it could have been worse. Once I am able to go to Jeff's trauma room, I see that he's being attended to by various hospital staff. Although he is barely able to speak, he lets me know that he's okay. Still concerned, we all stay with him for the rest of the night.

In the morning, I am the chosen one to drive the twenty miles to Norwalk, pickup my mother from work and to tell her of this occurrence. After telling her, I tried to assure her that Jeff is okay, but that did not stop the color from quickly leaving her face. Looking like

BLACK & BLUE IN BRIDGEPORT

she was about to faint, I knew she was worried. The only thing left to do was to pull off and drive her to the hospital, so she could see for herself. I wanted to stay, but I had an appointment I could not miss, so I left again hoping to make it to my destination on time.

Along with about twelve hundred other testers packed into Bridgeport's Central High School, I sat in a waiting area trying to prepare myself to take the City of Bridgeport's Civil Service Exam #1974. This test was only the first part of the full exam, but I needed to pass so that I could move forward in the process. As I sat, I knew I wasn't focused on what I had to do. I couldn't get my thoughts off Jeff and his condition. Looking around the room and realizing the sheer number of people on site, also began to discourage me. I fought off the negative feelings and agreed with myself that Jeff was in good hands and I needed to get my head right. I took a moment to refocus. Telling myself that I knew I wasn't a quitter and today wasn't going to be any different. I got it together and made myself ready to forge ahead.

After we were shuttled into the cafeteria of the building, we were then seated and administered the first part of the exam. This part was the written portion, but before we wrote a thing, we were given a series of wanted posters. As we looked at the posters, we were told to study them and to take mental notes of the information they displayed. After a brief period, all the posters were collected and then the questioning began. There were many questions about what the posters told us and then some questions about the city's geographical logistics as well. Finishing this part of the exam took roughly four hours and it was grueling, tedious and boring.

As I handed in my paperwork, I stopped to take a good look around the room. I looked at as many faces as I could and tried to commit each face to memory. If we all progressed in this process together, I wanted to remember them from this day. Quickly I noticed one of my roommates from college, Joey Gantt. I was happy to see him taking the test as well. During my sophomore year at Norfolk State, we were inseparable. It was like he and I against the world. We dated girlfriends, played ball, partied, shared majors and even an apartment together, off campus. Toward the end of the school year, Joe decided he wasn't coming back that following year and he left for Bridgeport a few weeks before final exams. At the end of the semester, I came home and although we were still friends, it was clear that we were moving in different directions.

When our test scores for this part of the exam were announced, I was relieved to have scored an 84.90. This wasn't the top score, but it wasn't the worse either. People with prior Military Service, like Joey, received additional points and that worked out great for him. Because of the high number of people taking the test, my score landed me at spot number 616 on the civil service waiting list. Joey scored higher than me and that put him in the first group to move forward into the first academy class. As for me, just having a little over eight years under my belt meant not enough time invested to retire or to earn a pension, so back to the telephone company I went.

What I did not know was there were new things on the horizon at SNET for me. I was promoted from a general office clerk in New Haven to a Business Representative working out of the city of Stamford. This promotion meant we had to move and that lead us to buying a new house. The new position, the home and new surroundings made for a good mix and it all made me happy.

Because of the move, I was reunited with a very good friend, Russell Payton. We had been teammates on the telephone company's basketball team and had won championships together. Seeing Russell brought back a lot of good memories. Mr. Inside and Mr. Outside is what we were called. Back then, I enjoyed playing for the company's team and we had a pretty good group of guys that made up our team. Winning most of our games, we often went to a bar afterwards to have a beer or two. We would all sit around and talk about all of the things that happened during our games, who played well, who didn't and who

BLACK & BLUE IN BRIDGEPORT

we were playing next week. One of our point guards from New Haven was Pee Wee. On one occasion he brought a female friend with him to a game that we won and she tagged along to the bar. While there, a conversation started about an event she had gone to at Yale University and she had pictures that she passed around for us to view. In one of the pictures I saw this beautiful woman that really sparked my interest, so I asked her about her. She told me that she was a really good friend, so I asked her to bring her to a game so that I could meet her in person.

At our following week's game, Pee Wee's friend walks into the gym and right there at her side is the beauty from the pictures. Avoiding wasting time, I walk right over to Pee Wee's friend and she smiles at me as she introduces me to her friend Yvette. I smile at Yvette and thank her for coming to the game. I step aside to let them go to find seats and I walk out onto the court as the game was about to start. I do not remember what team we were playing against, but we quickly took the lead and were winning and I was having a pretty good night. What I do remember is how I tried, with every chance I got, to look over where Yvette was sitting while I was playing. I could not help myself. I had to look because she was just that beautiful.

We won the game and that meant we were all heading to the Stratford Bowling Alley's bar for beers, some food and to celebrate. After arriving and finding a table for all of us to sit, I continued to enjoy every glance of Yvette that I could get. I was anxious to get into conversation with her and get to know her, so I looked directly at her whenever I talked. I even directed some of my comments at her, but she really didn't bite. There were carnival games upstairs and we all decided to go up and play a few. After awhile and several failed attempts to spark a real conversation with Yvette, I was starting to think this was how the night would end.

Then I took the chance and just started to talk. I told her how seeing her in the pictures the week before made me ask to meet her at the next game. My thought was after hearing how interested I was in her, maybe she would have some interest in me. Following my confession, not only did Yvette remain uninterested, she added not being impressed by me at all. I am not sure how it happened, but she gave me her number anyway and I promised to call her. What I did not know about that night, but later found out was that I was not her type. It seemed that Yvette's friend had lied to her in describing me. She was told that I was dark skinned, but in fact I was very much light skinned. To make matters worse, I was eight years older than her and I was still married.

Just hearing Mr. Inside and Mr. Outside still made me smile. Russell was six feet and three inches tall and weighed about two hundred and thirty pounds. He was big and strong, but his physical inside presence on the court and his exceptional leaping ability is what made him a great player. He was one of the most intimidating players in the whole Industrial Leagues. During that same time, I had found my outside shot and this let me chuck them with the best of them, from a good distance. Russ and I played together for about seven years in Bridgeport, New Haven and Stamford. We played hard together and that rewarded us with wins of two league championships. The first was the internal Telephone Company Statewide Tournament. This one featured teams from other SNET locations all over the state of Connecticut. The other team that made it to the championship game with us was from a Hartford location. They boasted a few ex-collegiate players and had dominated the tournament for the last five years. We barely beat them, but beat them we did. Both of our teams were named to the all-tournament team as well.

Although I was still interested in pursuing Yvette, I held back from calling her as much as I could, but I eventually did make that call. Even over the phone she still did not seem interested, but that made me desire her all the more. Over time, we talked a few more times and she even came to a few more games and then we got to know each other a little better. Ironically, she had actually just started working at the telephone company as well, up in New Haven. At my age then, I was not old, but Yvette made me feel younger. She had no children at the time and hanging out with her good friends, meant the world to her. She was laid back, chilled and not too serious about life yet and her powerful free spirit was perfectly matched with her seamless beauty. Although she had me on the hook, after talking off and on for a few weeks I started thinking things between us were not going anywhere, so maybe I should just back off. I was not sure why, but still being married at the time did not make things easier for us.

Then there was a Saturday that I went to New Haven to play ball at Goffee Street Park. While I was trying to find a place to park, I saw another girl that I had a brief relationship with in my past. When she saw me, she was surprised but also concerned. After I parked my car, I realized why. She was at the court with her old boyfriend whom we had had a run in over her, back when we were dating. She may have thought that I was going to have some issue with seeing them there, but I ignored them and played ball for a while, then decided to call Yvette. Once on the phone, Yvette told me that she was home and that she lived close to the park. After getting directions to her house, I stopped by and we really talked. She told me that she did like me, but she also confirmed my suspicion. Yvette then explained that she had a serious problem with me still being married. Although I shared that things were not going so well at home, I understood and wanted to respect her position, so we decided to just stay in touch. At this point I was not sure how things would be between Yvette and I, but I was sure that I wanted us to continue to talk.

That following year in the Industrial League, ironically, the Bridgeport Police Department's team became the team we had to beat in the playoffs. In our first match up during the season, Russell played a great game, but I shot the ball poorly and the police department took that win. During the second game, I found my rhythm. Shooting the ball better and sinking my shots, I was able to help our team and we took the win. At season's end, our team and the police department's team had identical 9-1 records. That meant we had to face them again in a third game to find out who was going to finally be named the league champions.

Just before the start of that final game, I was excited and let a few of the officers know that I might be playing on their team soon. I explained that I had taken the police exam and was currently on the waiting list. This news, I thought, would be of great interest to them, but instead, it was met by blank stares.

Never the less, that night Russell and I came together and put on one of the greatest offensive showings ever seen in that league. We came to play that night. We gave it all we had, while the officers watched us work the court on the inside and outside. When Russell wasn't dunking on them, I was peppering them with three-pointers. By the time we started the second half, the police department was trailing us by fifteen points.

That's when the gloves came off and they started playing dirty. Trying to send a message, we were treated to a few intentional hard fouls. Even so, they were unable to stop Russell from scoring. Next, they tried to isolate me to prevent me from getting the ball. When that didn't work, they tried the box-in-one defense on me. One of their players stayed in my face, following me all over the court bumping and pushing, as I tried to free myself up for shots. I admit, I was getting frustrated, but I was not going to let them stop me.

By now, I had about twenty points myself and their team calls for a time out. I then overheard one of their players say that he could stop me. When the game resumed, I made a quick cut to the basket and Russell passed me the ball. I could see their defender running toward me aggressively. He was trying to beat me to a spot on the court that he knew I was trying to get too. I stopped, dropped my shoulder into his chest and that propelled him backward to land on his ass on the floor. The referee blew his whistle on him for the foul. As I walked toward the foul line, he smiled at me and then a weird thing happened. Under his breath, he recited my car's license plate number to me.

I admit that I did not understand what that meant back then. After being on the job for a year, I came to understand the dirty trick. Back in those days, a police officer could get his hands on traffic ticket books that were not assigned to him. Using that unassigned book, he could then write out tickets and discard the part that is normally left on your windshield, but turn in the official copy. Intentionally, you would never know that you had been issued a ticket. As time passed, the fines would automatically double. Then to your surprise, you would get a letter from the police department threatening you to come in to pay.

These tickets were called sleepers and someone had written two on my car after we won the championship. What made me realize these tickets were sleepers is that they were issued to me at my home address. At home, I parked my car in the yard at the end of a long driveway and should have never got tickets there. I guess that was the punishment for our team winning that well over the police department's team that year. I even remember at the game's end, the players would not even shake our hands; they just walked off the court.

Playing basketball always excited me and playing on a team made me happy, but that year also had its low points because of all the loss. My second child, Taylor Mellissa, was born premature and she passed away after only living three months. My father, who had been fighting it, finally succumbed to lung cancer. While a good friend, Mike Scott, only twenty-four years old, was also taken by cancer.

Even with all the good changes that had happened at the job and at home and all the great games I had played, death and grieving can force anyone to slow down for a time. Although it was bad timing, the second part of the police officer's exam testing was announced. By now, my wife was worried and wondering if I should continue or not. This portion of the test was focused on physical agility. So I told my wife that I wanted to take the test, just to see how far I could go in the process. To try to put her at ease, I also explained that I did not plan on taking the job, even if it was offered to me.

On the day of the test, I breezed through all the parts; agility, psychological, lie detector and the drug testing. A few days passed and the next letter arrived announcing the upcoming doctor's physical that would be taken six days later. That night, my mother's only brother Donald M. Crockett passed away from cancer in North Carolina. Two days later I was on Interstate 95 South, heading to Winston-Salem, North Carolina to attend my uncle's funeral.

After driving to North Carolina myself, I was wakening from a short nap when my aunt's niece Kirstin and her family were just arriving. We were introduced for the first time and it seemed a little weird, but we were immediately attracted to one another. Kirstin was a nurse, working at Yale Hospital, back in New Haven, Connecticut. She and I both spent the rest of the day sneaking peaks and smiling at each other.

That night when sleeping arrangements were being discussed for the twenty or so people staying at my uncle's house, I asked my aunt where I would be sleeping. Without warning, Kirstin says out loud, you can sleep with me. I turned totally red. Looking around the room towards my mother for her reaction, but she pretended she had not heard it. My aunt didn't pretend at all, just smiled. I was totally embarrassed. I played it off and didn't follow up on the advance. Later that day, I was out in the back yard shooting some hoops. When I was done, I walked back toward the house and was met at the doorway with a towel. My aunt's niece wiped away my sweat and then massaged my shoulders for good measure. By the next day the sparks were flying everywhere for everyone to see. Finally, Kirstin and I made plans to see each other once we got back home. Eventually, I got myself together and we all attended the funeral. Afterward, I jumped in my car and drove all the way back to Connecticut to arrive just fifteen minutes before my scheduled physical for the police exam.

BLACK & BLUE IN BRIDGEPORT

The final step of the exam was the background check. I remember coming home from work and my neighbors telling me that they had been interviewed by the policemen about me. The next day, I would be called into the office at work to be told by my supervisor about a police detective questioning her about my work habits and job history. Given glowing reports by all, the police department then turned and offered me the position of a police officer within the department.

I had a long talk with my wife and my mother where I expressed my strong desire to take the police job. My wife knew I wasn't happy at the telephone company and that I really wanted to work with children. She cautiously agreed to the idea of me taking the job, but I had to promises. I promised not to become a narc or vice cop and that I wouldn't needlessly put myself in harm's way. After this, she agreed and I was given her blessing.

My mother, on the other hand, was very quiet. I could feel her anguish and I knew she was worried. She simply said, "If that's what you want to do." Although I expected more, I came to realize that all my achievements throughout the whole process and finally being offered the job would ultimately be my only undertaking my mother never bragged about.

For me, having both of them with me on this was very, very important to me. What they thought and felt about me becoming a police officer carried a lot of weight with me and made a big difference. I will never be sure if they knew, but had either one of them stayed dead set against it, I would not have proceeded. I would have refused the job and never became a police officer. Even though in my heart, I had wanted nothing more.

As time passed and thoughts of Yvette always on my mind, I was still going through the rigorous steps of becoming a Bridgeport Police Officer at the same time. Surprisingly, Yvette and I did continue to talk. In fact, we started seeing more of each other. I started making weekly trips to New Haven and we would meet at events and parties in the area. Over time, I met most of her friends and many of her family members as well. Eventually and without big fanfare, our spending time together developed into a relationship.

After separating from my first wife, I left Bridgeport and moved to the city of West Haven. After my divorce was final, Yvette moved in with me. I never thought anything could have made me happier than Yvette agreeing to live together, but I was wrong. In what seemed no longer than a beautiful moment, Yvette blessed me by having my son David Daniels IV. A few years following David, my daughter Deja Yvonne arrived and Yvette and I had a family. The only thing left to make it official was marriage and that we both agreed on.

Yvette and I both said I do and became husband and wife, but by now the tide of happiness and bliss was turning. Nothing was just about her or me anymore, because there were children to be raised. Once we married, it seemed as if we could never agree on anything. Slowly I began to notice how we saw the world in totally different ways. I could never really say how things got so out of control, but what I can say is that there was a lot of passion and pain that span over a lot of years.

In the end, things really got rough for us and Yvette was tougher than I could have ever imagined. Although she made me feel like I faced every fear a man could face in a relationship with a woman, I am sure it was just as hard for her. Ironically for me, things had really turned upside down when I started to feel like the things that drew me closer to her were now the things that were pushing me away. After making five attempts to live together that only succeeded in five separations, we both had to finally accept what was inevitable. Over time, I came to understand that the beauty that I had seen in the pictures was no longer the woman standing next to me. At ebb tide, it became a situation bereft of feelings. There was never a formal goodbye from either of us, just a perpetual retreat to neutral corners to escape the pain. For as beautiful and free as Yvette was back when I met her, she remains to this day, from a distance.

BLACK & BLUE IN BRIDGEPORT

While my relationship had ended, that phone call I had been waiting on finally came. There were about thirty of us got that call to come and start our training. When we showed up, we were ushered into a room, given bottles to urinate into that would be drug tested on the spot. We were then led to a bathroom and our samples were collected. From here, we were told that we would be starting soon, but for now to just go home.

The results of the drug tests did dwindle down the thirty that were called, but on October 31, 1989 at 8 a.m. sharp, I was one of the citizens that entered the doors of The Bridgeport Police Academy at 280 Tesiny Avenue. Here is where I would start my official training to become what I had always wanted to become. It had been a little over a year of waiting to get into the academy, but the timing was perfect. Now I had ten years invested at SNET and that made me pension eligible.

After hiding my desire, getting all the negative reactions and just waiting for what almost seemed like forever, today marked the day everything would change. Today, I, David Daniels, III took my last step into finally realizing my dream.

Chapter III
The Prospect Inception

Part of the New England region, Bridgeport, Connecticut is about thirty miles north of the New York state line. Also known as the Park City, Bridgeport continues to hold its position as the largest populated city in the state. Covering about eighteen square miles in America's second richest county, Bridgeport is just shy of boosting one hundred forty-seven thousand people, including myself, living and calling Bridgeport their home. It's minority population, mostly consisting of Hispanics, Blacks, Asians and Jamaicans.

Its nickname, The Park City, came about because of the creation and donation of its two major parks; Seaside and Beardsley. Back in 1990, Bridgeport also made its mark by holding the top spot for the northeastern states in murders per capita. On a national scale, the city took fifth place for most stolen cars in a year. As for unemployment, when I started writing this book in 1995 and even to this year of 2019, Bridgeport's high unemployment rates still reign supreme. I know it all sounds gloomy, but either way, Bridgeport still remains my home town. I was born here and I know of a time when things didn't look so uninviting.

In the late 1940's and early 1950's, Bridgeport was known as a booming industrial center because of its high number of big factories.

BLACK & BLUE IN BRIDGEPORT

Carpenter Steel, Jenkins Valves, The Bead Chain Company, Bridgeport Brass and General Electric, to name a few. These companies employed thousands of workers. This made getting a job plentiful for almost anyone that was searching. These options are some of the reasons so many people came to Bridgeport in the first place, including my parents.

Their story starts back in the mid-fifties. In search of jobs and a better life, my parents joined in on a mass movement happening across the United States called the great migration. During this migration, large numbers of African Americans moved from the rural southern states to the urban northeast, Midwest and western states in America. At its conclusion, almost six million black people, along with my parents, had also made this journey to find new lives and homes up north.

They were mostly attracted to the bright lights of New York City. Although their paths from the cities of Winston-Salem and Greenville, out of North Carolina were different, both my parents ultimately landed here. Here in this sparsely lit, less expensive place called New England is where the jobs were. These jobs were the type that could lead to better lives.

My father, David Daniels, Jr. was a strong and proud black man when he arrived in Bridgeport those many years ago. He had served in the Army in the Korean conflict and was now a Veteran. Although I have to admit he was stubborn, more importantly, he was a loving and caring father. He stood about six feet tall and was known to be a bit of a lady's man. He wore his hair slicked back, loved to hang out at the bars and being with his friends. For work, he was an inspector and steel worker at Carpenter's Steel. When he wasn't at work, he enjoyed playing the piano, being an auto mechanic and was a pretty good artist. I remember how much he loved to draw.

My mother, Jean Carolyn Crockett is a God fearing, outspoken, industrious black woman. She loves her children with all her heart

DAVID DANIELS, III

and soul and was our rock growing up. A great cook, very creative, community oriented and truly could make a dollar out of fifteen cents. She is short, light skinned with curly hair and glasses that let her see the world very clearly. Although she was a little woman and very caring, she was not a push over. She would cuss you out, if you wanted to take it there and give it to you better than any man could.

Here in Bridgeport is where they met, fell in love and married. That same love produced six healthy children: Deborah, David, III, Reggie, Carolyn Janine, Jeffery and Donald. In the beginning and for a modicum time, we lived in an apartment on Wordin Avenue. Just two blocks from the West Side Park that sits directly across the street from the well known P.T. Barnum Housing Apartments.

My father, who did love us, also had other loves. He loved to hang out with his friends and to drink alcohol, especially beer. Unfortunately for us all, the day came when enjoying his other loves changed our lives forever. One of my father's drinking buddies was also his oldest brother William. To us, he was Uncle Bud.

During a regular night of drinking, a fight with one of his other drinking buddies broke out and ended with the death of my uncle. My father reacted to the pain of Uncle Bud's death poorly and left him only wanting to be drunk and that was most of the time. As time passed, he seemed to slowly withdraw from life and our family. This led to many arguments between him and my mother. Those arguments led to him abusing her and the abuse led to him not being around at all for us. Sadly, we had to watch him turn into a bitter and cold man.

While we were still living on Wordin Avenue, things got a lot harder. It's easy remembering a time when there was no heat in the middle of a New England winter and how my mother kept the house warm with the stove and burners always on. One day, my younger brother Reggie and I, were in the kitchen because it was cold in the house. I was sitting at the table and he was standing real close to the open stove.

"You better get back away from that stove Reggie."
I say to him, because I didn't want him to get burnt.
"But I'm cold, I'm really cold!"
Reggie yells back at me as he turns around from the stove to face me, while continuing to rub his hands together.

Before I say another word, his shirt tail drags on the oven door and bursts into flames. I jump up as Reggie hears the fire start and looks behind himself to see his shirt on fire.

"No!"

He yells in a panic and takes off running through the house.

Running behind him, I wrestle him to the floor. Rolling him around and trying to put the fire out, I try to calm him down with my voice.

"You okay Reggie. You gonna be alright, keep rolling over. It's going out. You're going to be okay!"

I tried my best to put the fire out quick, but it wasn't quick enough. After calling 911 for help, Reggie ended up going to Park City Hospital. Being there for burns he sustained at home wasn't a good thing for us and it exposed our living conditions. But what happened next made living without heat seem easy. I remember over hearing the social worker telling my mother.

"I'm sorry Mrs. Daniels, but I have no choice."

My mother tried to fight it, but in the end, the state decided that our living conditions were not conducive to raising two small children. As a result, my two youngest brothers were taken and placed into foster care. It would be two long years before they came home.

Around that time is when I realized the loving and caring father we all knew, had completely faded away. He seemed to only show up to argue and abuse my mother. Finally, feeling like our family unit was destroyed, my mother and father separated for good. I remember leaving that apartment. Just my mother, with us in tow, left like thieves in the night. She hid us with various friends and relatives until we eventually landed in The P.T. Barnum Housing Projects in a two bedroom unit and on Welfare.

Named after Phineas T. Barnum of The Barnum & Bailey Circus, the P.T. Barnum Housing Projects is a low income housing development. This development was built on a tract of land that for some years before, served as the old fair grounds for the circus. Here is where the circus lions, tigers and elephants were quartered during the winter months. At some point, the land was secured by the city. What was set to be built in 1950 were twenty-two buildings, with most being three floors each, all red bricked with more than two hundred fifty units. After moving in, we quickly learned that outsiders only referred to P.T. Barnum Housing Projects as just 'the projects.' But for those of us living here, we also affectionately called it P.T.

As time passed, I realized that P.T. had an economy all its own. If you needed money, you didn't have to go far. You could borrow it from within the P.T. neighborhood, from a loan shark. Needed liquor after hours? You find and visit any one of the plenty bootleggers around. The same applied for drugs, candy, women and even clothes. Even if you wanted to put in a bet on the dog races, you could find someone within the buildings that was taking bets. Almost anything could be had for the right price. Once you found the right person, in the right building, anyone could get what they were looking for.

With six children in our household, there seemed to never be enough of anything to go around. Clothes, money, food or just about anything was spread thin. My mother tried and did her best with very limited resources. Our cabinets and refrigerator were bare most of the month. We did eat every day, but it still seemed like we were always hungry. Just as fast as my mother would put food and provisions in place, they were quickly depleted.

In those early years my mother did what everyone called days work. This is work that's done under the table, meaning she got paid in cash. This kind of work usually came around from white folks looking to get cheap labor. She would get up and go work where the rich people lived, in Westport. Many families living in P.T. worked like this to help supplement their meager welfare checks. Depending on how well my mother worked and if the people cared about her, there were perks.

I can remember my mother bringing home hand me downs of clothes and old toys from them. Their cast-offs seemed to be better than most of the stuff we already had. We use to be happy to see my mother bringing in bags of stuff. But then, there was also the welfare lady. She was a state worker coming into our home to check our closets to see if any man was living with us. She made a monthly visit to our home to do that inspection. I use to watch her looking in our pantry and other places that I thought were private, but that's the way it was done.

When your family is on welfare, as a child, I never wanted to get sick or need medical treatment. If any one of us did, my mother would have to take us to the welfare building. In the times I had to go there, I remember it being a dreadful place. Housed in a city owned building that sat at the foot of Main Street and Madison Avenue, it was a dark and dank brick building. On arrival, we would be ushered into this reception area like cattle.

On television I was exposed to the wonderful bedside manner of Dr. Kildare and Ben Casey. But in real life, we had none of that. The doctors and nurses that treated us at the welfare building had little compassion and seemed to have less regard for our health. They consistently wore soiled white uniforms along with their mean facial expressions. These trips to the welfare building, that we had no choice but to take continue to linger as some of my worst childhood memories. That place was a house of horrors and didn't fall short of a torture chamber for children. Those experiences would taint and encumber my relationship with doctors and dentist even into my adulthood.

DAVID DANIELS, III

By default, my older sister Deborah was often left in charge of watching over us younger ones, because my mother had to work. My sister, being a free spirit, quickly began to reject this way of life for herself. She became unruly with my mother and started running away. She would be gone for days and sometimes weeks at a time. Many times, she would return for a while and then would be gone again. Because I was just a year younger, but yet a little more stable, my siblings became my charges. I willingly watched over them. I made sure they were fed with whatever we had in the house and loved on them until my mother returned. Although his aggravation wasn't about being left at home with the rest of us, my younger brother Reggie finally became a malcontent. He got fed up about being without and always hungry. Tired of just waiting and getting only what was given to him, he began taking what he wanted.

Even though our environment could be so depressing, because of the violence and general poverty, I still liked growing up there. It was my home and my friends and I called it my hood. Yes we were poor, when it came to having money, but that made us no different than most of the other families living in P.T. at that time. Where I found my happiness was in the people and the families. All of the black folks were everywhere and so many different personalities to experience. So many characters that were always entertaining and each of them having so many unique attitudes.

Families like the Bohannons. Ms. Bohannon made the best cakes in the projects. I guess it was easy, because she was always baking for their fourteen kids. Then there were the Jacksons. They were a big family that reminded me of the Cartwrights from the television show, Bonanza. They came here from Manning, South Carolina and boy could they tell a scary ghost story. Their stories would have you scared to go to bed for two weeks. As it seemed, life in our hood revolved around the biggest families and what they were doing. Then there were the Geters. They had relatives all over town, mostly boys. Most were six footers and were respected and feared at the same time. The twenty-two buildings that made up P.T. Barnum Apartments was somewhat split in half by the drive. The drive was a one-way single lane car path that started up by the rental office and let out down by the basketball courts.

Over the years, I spent most of my time playing basketball, chasing girls and hanging on the drive with my friends. Sometimes there was fighting and getting beat up, but most of the time we were partying and listening to music. At the age of thirteen, I fell in love with music and started buying vinyl records like I was crazy.

During those formative years, we lived in apartment 308 on the third floor in building thirteen out in P.T. Building thirteen was located in the middle of the complex and all the buildings looked identical. Built in the shape of a wide U, each building had a concrete courtyard out front that it shared with the aligned building facing it. There were concrete benches, mental pole clothes lines and a concrete water sprinkler that the children could play in during the summer months. The two entry doors per building led to stairwells that went all the way up to the third floors. Twelve apartments to each hallway meant twelve families in our building.

On the first floor of our building lived the Lemdons. They were Muslim and were one of the few families in the projects that had a father in the home. Mr. Jerry worked for the city and did photography on the side. His wife, Mrs. Iris would kick us out of their kitchen when she was making bean pies or carrot cakes, as the recipes were closely guarded secrets.

They spoke openly about Black Muslim doctrine. Which at the time, was centered on self-help for black people and about a war they called Armageddon. In this war, blacks would fight and defeat the white people, which they called the devils of the United States of America. Quite often they would invite me to accompany them to the Temple where they would go to worship. Even though I wanted to go,

DAVID DANIELS, III

just to be near their daughter Sheddi, I never did. All the war talk was way too radical for me.

In the projects, we only saw policemen come into the neighborhood to arrest, harass, intimidate, scare or brutalize someone. These policemen always were white and I didn't see a black policeman until I was about eleven years old.

The first time I seen a black cop was almost a surprise to me, right in P.T. A patrol car was parked near building four and I wandered over because it was surrounded by kids. I peered into the open window and saw this soft spoken black man with a small afro protruding from under his police cap. He was polite to us. He answered all of our questions and even let us turn-on the siren and strobe lights. We were talking on the loudspeaker before the radio beckoned him to another call and off he went into the night. It was inspiring to see a police officer that showed us that he was a person too. In our quick interaction, he even showed us that he cared about how he treated us. The fact that he was black made it stick in my memory even more. I could never forget that moment in time, because it made me think that I could also be a policeman one day.

Radicalism and revolution were the catchphrases of the day back then, so much was going on. Just a few years back there were a host of assassinations the country had experienced. Malcolm X, Martin Luther King, Jr. and the Kennedys, all assassinated. I remember hearing things like 'I knew this was going to happen,' and 'You can't go around talking about the white man like that.'

As a response, two things began to happen. The drug culture exploded and it seemed like drug selling and abuse were running rampant. This gave the police a reason to come out in a heightened presence. Police officers and patrol cars were everywhere. They were like an occupying force during wartime and that made it easy to understand why so many people I knew and saw everyday were going to jail.

BLACK & BLUE IN BRIDGEPORT

Even though I was young, I understood why certain people were being arrested by the white cops that seemed to always be in our hood. What I did not understand was why arresting someone had to be so violent and demeaning. Most were mistreated, if not they were dealt with in a less than humane manner. When I was twelve or so, I remember.

One afternoon the police came to arrest this older kid, he was about eighteen or nineteen. He struggled and resisted them, because he didn't want to go to jail. In turn, the police beat him mercilessly. These two white cops hit him with black jacks, sprayed him with mace and all the while calling him every kind of nigger in the book. They then dragged him, in handcuffs out of the building into the courtyard and threw him into the back of a police car. They did all of that in plain view of the crowd that gathered to see what all the commotion was about. They treated him like they were taking out a bag of trash.

Then there was the drug dealer. He was in his early twenties. He was a drug dealer and what we called a hustler out in P.T. When the police came for him, it was a little different. Although he didn't struggle and resist, he had a strong will to be free. He didn't fight with them, but broke free about six times and ran off trying to get away. Every time they caught up to him, they would beat on him. They chased him all over the complex for about twenty minutes. In the end the results were the same. Ultimately he was thrown in the back of a police car in a swollen and bloody heap.

Then, there were The Black Panthers. Almost appearing out of nowhere, the Black Panthers started to emerge in our hood. Posters of their jailed leader Huey P. Newton could be seen everywhere. This black and white picture showed him seated in a wicker chair with a pump shotgun in one hand and a spear in the background. This picture had a cold imposing quality to it and left an indelible impression in my mind. With their trademark light blue shirts, jeans, combat boots and

DAVID DANIELS, III

black leather jackets replete with 'Free Huey' buttons, they marched in their free breakfast program and cut quite a presence in the hood. They were always saying "Burn baby Burn." They spoke about H. Rap Brown and Eldridge Cleaver and others leading the struggle to help poor and black people. They sold Panther Papers which featured a ten point program for change. It had a caricature of a policeman as a pig stating that cops were always playing the victim of unprovoked attacks.

During this time, P.T. became a hotbed of activity and I remember a large contingent of whites coming in and being around. They were all with the Peace Corps. Some were hippies, church missionaries and others worked on a film documentary crew. They took over one of the apartments, setup inside and began what they called missionary works. They tried to educate and organize the youth and made lots of political statements. They were everywhere, but it did not make a difference for us or the police. I remember walking to get a pizza from Beverly's Pizza House, which was in a white neighboring area called Black Rock. As I was walking, I heard someone yell 'go back to the projects where you came from.' When I turned and looked, it was a police officer.

In the mist of all this negativity, there was also a renewal of black pride and Afro-centricity. This made blacks all over start to try and think positive and maybe do better, but not my father. My parents were separated by this time, but my father would come over drunk just to raise hell. On many occasions, the police would be called to remove him from the premises. As my father's drinking got worse, his interaction with the police increased. Letting his driver's license get suspended brought Big Frank into his life. Big Frank was one of the officers that would pull him over repeatedly. He never arrested my father. Instead, he would let him go with the promise that he would come over Frank's house on Sundays and work his crime off by cleaning up his yard. This arrangement lasted for years. I even went with my father to help him clean up. After we were done, Big Frank would give my father five dollars and a pint of liquor for his efforts.

BLACK & BLUE IN BRIDGEPORT

WHEN I STARTED WRITING this book and trying to formulate ideas for what would become of this chapter, I was just a patrolman. Assigned an overtime shift, I was sent to a juvenile detention center called Meade Hall. Being here around the youth is what helped me to decide how to write about my childhood.

Here at the center right now, is a group of about twenty kids, mixed, male and female. Although they are young and have angelic features, they are alleged to have stolen cars, burglarized homes, displayed other anti-social behaviors or worse. I am here on this day to protect one of them whom was involved in a murder. This murder was perpetrated on someone with gang ties and that puts this young person in line for a hit on their life.

As I sit here and watch these kids posture, socialize, laugh and cry, I am reminded of my own youth. I am reminded of the good and the bad that was my environment growing up. I also remember how I knew that I wanted to be a policeman, but I suppressed my desires back then. I would not talk about it with anyone because the police had such a negative and adversarial relationship with my community.

There was no such thing as protect and serve back then. The police seemed to just be against the black and the poor. To make matters worse, groups like the Black Panthers, who tried to help, were named the number one internal threat in America by J. Edgar Hoover. He even developed a program called Cointelpro to eradicate the group. I later found out that Connecticut is centrally connected to the Black Panthers. John Huggins and Bobby Seale co-founded the group and John is from New Haven, Connecticut. Trying to do good works here, John, his wife Erica and Bobby were once indicted and tried for inciting a riot on The New Haven Green.

But this place, Meade Hall, also has a significant place in my memory. This is the very place my own brother was housed when he made his introduction into the criminal justice system. While Reggie started out taking things when he was young, it didn't stop there. It culminated into a life of larceny, drug abuse, murder and then prison in adulthood. Along the way it yielded him a black Probation Officer named Ernest L. Parker, who also befriended the whole family.

Mr. Parker played football with the legendary Leroy Kelly at Morgan State University in Baltimore, Maryland. He also worked in probation in Philadelphia in the 60's when gangs ruled that city. I remember him showing news clippings of all the violence involving the gang culture in Philadelphia and discouraging us from making bad choices in life. He was a positive force and ultimately became one of the biggest influences on my own life. Although he could not save Reggie, I believe I got lucky to have Mr. Parker in my life, because of my brother.

With little to no rehabilitation available, looking at jailed youth equals wasted lives and families torn apart. Our kids are just warehoused in places like this. That, I can relate to. My brother's odyssey within this system ended years later after he received a fifteen year bid for the murder of his then girlfriend. Even into my early twenties I was still suppressing my desire to become a cop. My new fear became facing the day I would have to arrest my own brother.

I could not just sit silent and watch the kids, I spoke to them. We spoke about their lives, about their crimes and I played ping pong with them. Spending time with them reminded me of that black officer that was there for us. I once shared my story of meeting my first black officer with a friend and I was surprised yet again. That friend proudly shared with me that my black officer was Officer Lafayette White, his brother.

The kids and I quickly moved to shooting some baskets. But they didn't know who they were messing with. Basketball is and will always be my favorite sport. I love the Philadelphia 76ers. They are my favorite professional team, even though they are not that same team which dominated the league in the 80's. Those great players like George

BLACK & BLUE IN BRIDGEPORT

McGinnis, Dr. J., Charles Barkley and Allen Iverson, are the reasons I still love visiting the Spectrum in Philadelphia to this day.

While the kids and I laughed and played, I wondered how many dreams and desires of becoming doctors, lawyers, politicians and even policeman were being chewed up by this system. Back in my time, I was shocked by what I saw from the police officers that came into my hood. But the desire to become a police officer was always burning inside even though I wasn't ready to share that revelation with the world. My hope was playing and laughing with a police officer could just maybe start or keep their desires alive.

The fact still remains, that in the projects, where most of these children live, there are a lot of negative role models. Prostitutes, drug dealers, users and many other criminal types, even police officers. Many years later, becoming an officer myself, I was in full uniform as I stood in line at Dunkin Donuts. The guy in front of me turned around to tell me that he was a retired cop himself. And now, he was living in Florida. I told him I remembered him. He looked a little confused. So I then told him I remember what he had done to my father. Big Frank almost walked thru the window trying to get away from me and out the door that day. I was reminding him of his corruption. Using my father to clean up his yard all those Sundays for free was wrong and he knew it. He could have just arrested my father, but instead he chose to use the law for his personal gain.

Positive role models and safe environments matter for everyone, but more importantly for the kids. The struggle is real and I know. My positive role models and strong desires saved me. But I am still lucky. Lucky to have been able to pull from my youth the things that touched me, basketball and music. From those early days until today, my collection of music is eclectic and extensive. Encompassing; jazz, hip-hop, rap, rhythm and blues, new age and other genres as well. My love of music is what pushed me to becoming a DJ.

DAVID DANIELS, III

Easily, we all can see that there aren't a lot of positive role models for today's children. This isn't because they don't exist, it's because those whom survive this type of environment and become successful, abandon their roots and turn away.

But when I turn, I turn toward these kids of today. I see them and I see myself. Although I can't reach into their lives and pluck them out of their environmental nightmares, I am there for them. In the end, I just want to be someone. Someone they see as a man, a police officer or just that friend that inspires them to doing the right things in life and to living their best lives.

Chapter IV
Becoming Blue
Hidden Costs

Lieutenant David Boston stood in front us all packed into an old grammar school auditorium on the cities' north end. My classmates and I listening intently as the commander of the facility commanded our attention. He welcomed us into the profession. Told us it was the world's largest fraternity and that our lives would never be the same, here after. He explained how the world would now hold us to higher standard and that we would be forfeiting some our rights in that process. For me, it was a very scary speech and I began to wonder, had I made the right decision by taking this job.

My classmates were black, white, Hispanic, male and female alike. In the mix, we had two veteran officers retraining with us. There was William (Ronnie) Bailey and my old college roommate Joey Gantt. Officer Bailey was being punished with retraining for having gotten himself into some sort of trouble within the department. While Joey, he had graduated in the class before me but was short in mandated hours in report writing and emergency medical response. Two other recruits were already working for the police departments of Shelton and Stratford Connecticut. Two other classmates were sister and brother and they were both married to veteran officers. There were a few cop kids in our class and even a former police dispatcher. But for the most of us, we came from everyday jobs like; factory workers, hair dressers, a radio disc jockey, cable television worker and even from the telephony company. That first day was pretty much uneventful and mostly about us checking each other out, while the staff was probably checking us all out.

We were outfitted with beige khaki uniforms replete, black belts and boots with only the Bridgeport police department shoulder patch standing out that made up our everyday wear. Some of my classmates had been in the military, which fell right in with the paramilitary training we were all about to receive. Each morning we stood inspection. The staff checked us out for things like breaches in cleanliness and/or order were noted. A couple of recruits quickly fell out of favor for being male with pierced ears and were ridiculed daily by the staff. One recruit Harold Dimbo took a daily barrage of insults and continued to wear his diamond stud, while others relented and stop wearing them all together.

Our instructional staff was mostly comprised of veteran department officers, with a few exceptions and they loved playing head games with us. On Mondays, we were a bunch of worthless plasma units, but on Fridays, we were getting closer to becoming Bridgeport Police officers. I think they used these methods so we didn't get into any trouble over the weekends. We were taught a wide range of subjects from; report writing, the Connecticut Penal Code, accident investigation, the laws of search and seizure, motor vehicle law, drunk driver procedures and emergency medical response, just to name a few. We were tested almost daily and had guest lecturers from; The Connecticut State Police, F.B.I., D.E.A., A.T.F. and other law enforcement agencies. We learned about weapons, counterfeit money and bombs. We were even visited and taught by the Secret Service.

We were introduced to each division within the police department itself. The Detective and Youth Bureaus, Patrol, the Community Services Division and apprised of all of their functions. I loved being in the academy, because there was so much to learn. Including watching all the different personalities of my classmates emerge. I would sit there and wonder what type of cops they were going to be.

We gave nicknames to some of our instructors based on their attitudes. We called our search and seizure instructor 'Robocop' because he never smiled and looked like he would arrest his own mother. We called our report writing instructor 'Dr. Bellows' because he acted like he knew a little bit about everything and was always sharing his opinion.

One day in class, Dr. Bellows told us that some of us were not even going to make it through the academy. He said that some of us were going to wind up getting in trouble, others would be investigated by Internal Affairs at some point during our career and that some of us would be fired before reaching retirement. Some of us would be hurt on the job, sued and yet others would be victimized by the very profession we had chosen to pursue. His speech was a very sobering speech. I think every last one of us went out and put all of our worldly possessions in our wives names afterwards.

One Monday morning instructor, Dr. Bellows, came into our classroom, closed the door, said hello and began to talk to us about the day's lesson. A short time later, a knock on the door interrupted the class. That two-seasoned officer that was retraining with us was asked to stand up and come out of the class into the hallway. Then Dr. Bellows was also beckoned into hallway. He steps out into the hallway and shuts the door behind himself. The rest of us sat there silently, not knowing what to do, other than looking around and wondering about what was going on.

From all the noise coming from the hallway, we could make out a woman's voice screaming at top of her lungs and arguing with Dr. Bellows. As Dr. Bellows opened the door to re-enter the classroom, he looked back out into the hallway and said.

"I'll talk to you later!"

That was it. Dr. Bellows closed the door and resumed teaching. Walking around the class as he spoke to us, he paused in front of my desk as the classroom's door flew back open. A young white female stepped into the doorway, looked directly at Dr. Bellows and screamed.

"You bastard!"

Then she raised a pistol and started firing shots at Dr. Bellows. He fell to the floor and pandemonium ensued. I was seated right in the front row when the shooting started. I dove all the way to the wall, nearly fifteen feet away to the back of that row. When I looked up, all I saw were bodies piled on top of each other all over the room. My classmates were all on the floor in every nook and cranny in the room and a few of them had even made it out of the room. Dr. Bellows was still in the front of the room, lying face down and perfectly still. Before anyone of us could speak about what just happened, Dr. Bellows jumped up off the floor. He dusted himself off and said.

"I want a report on what just happened. The whole thing had been staged for your benefit."

He then looked directly at me, winked and said.

"Recruit Daniels! Your report should be the shortest and easiest to write, because I know that all most of you saw, was the back wall and the feet of some of your classmates."

Then, he began to laugh.

Another day was bomb day in class. After returning from our lunch break, we see an elaborate table display of testing bombs setup. All types of bombs that The Connecticut State Police had sent down with a trooper to instruct us on. There were pipe bombs and dynamite stick bombs for all of us to look at. As me and my classmates perused over the information listed at each device, I was fascinated by the devices. I paused at a rather interesting one and then, without thinking, I picked it up. By doing that, touching it, I triggered its mercury switch and a flashbulb lit up and scared me shitless. Looking over at me and reaction, everyone laughed at me. I learned a valuable lesson that day about touching things and I would be reminded of it.

After I had been on the job nearly a year and was at Park City Hospital on a call, a nurse walked up to me, looked at my name tag and started laughing hysterically. As I stood and watched her, she tried to say something but her laughing made it hard to understand. Once she could get the words out, she tells me that her husband was the bomb expert that had visited the academy that day. She goes on to say that her husband decided to name that bomb after me because of how funny my reaction was and then she walked away, still laughing at me.

That same week, I found out what happens when we show up and our uniforms are not up to standards. In my haste to get there on time, I forgot my belt. During our morning inspection, the instructor noticed my situation and I told him that at lunchtime I would drive home to retrieve it. He looked at me, told me he had a better idea and then he walked off and disappeared. When he returned, he had a piece of rope. As he handing it to me, he told me to wear that as a belt for the rest of the day. Every one of my classmates got a kick out of that. I could hear them snickering and calling me 'Jethro' as I passed them by. Of course, I never forgot my belt again after that and it only took a few weeks to figure out most of the head games they were playing with us. From that point forward, I was no longer intimidated, but sometimes I still needed to be taken down a peg or two.

Three months at the academy had passed and the upcoming water rescue training was announced. I had been dreading this day, because I didn't know how to swim. Some of my classmates told the instructors that they didn't know how to swim also. They were told that if they couldn't swim they would be thrown into nine feet of water anyway. That response brought the room to silence. All week long the rumors persisted that they were going to throw us in the water. I told one of my classmates that I could not swim and that if anyone threw me in nine feet of water they better hope that I drown. I said that if I made it out of the water I was going to kick that person's ass, quit the academy and just return to the telephone company. My classmate quietly said that he couldn't swim either. I directed him to stay close to me and that we would be okay.

That Friday afternoon came and we all were transported to The Cardinal Shehan Center to complete our water safety instruction. We arrived at the facility, hit the locker room to change into our bathing suits and then were ushered into the pool area. Some of my classmates that could swim immediately jumped into the pool to show off. They were all over that pool. Using the driving board, doing flips and cartwheels as the rest of us just stood there looking at each other then back at the water.

With a big entrance comes the department instructors and they quickly lined us all up. My classmate, that I told to stay near me, positioned himself right next to me. I dug in my heels and clenched my fist and waited for whatever was going to happen next. We were divided into two groups, the swimmer and the non-swimmers. The instructors sent the non-swimmers, my group, to the low end of the pool and made us get in the water. That was it. No pushing us into the deep end or anything threatening. Most of the women were down where I was and we basically played in the water as my stress about the situation melted away. I hadn't actually been in a pool in years, so I actually enjoyed thrashing around in the water. The other male recruit stayed right at my side the whole time.

Next up was the State Police Training Facility in Meriden, Connecticut for the defensive driving course. Divided into groups of nine recruits each, we were assigned an instructor and then he drove through the obstacle course to show us what had to be done. Each recruit had to maneuver through the same course, but under pressure to pass the course. In my group, I drove first.

Along with me in the car would be the instructor in the passenger seat and two other recruits in the back seat. After I sat behind the wheel in the cruiser, the instructor activated the overhead lights, the sirens and start wildly screaming at me. I needed to take off driving about eighty feet ahead into a pool of water called the splash pad, where there were two safety cones set up. At the cones, I had to make a sharp right turn which caused the now wet tires to skid and the cruiser went into a fishtail. After recovering control of the cruiser, I would have to park it between two other cones set up a few feet away. I made it to the end and for me, it was fun.

Also in my group was that recruit that I'd protected in the pool, Ernie Grasso and he was the last to drive. While he drove, I sat in the back with another recruit and we had no idea what was about to happen. After the instructor hit the lights and siren, the driver took off. He did hit the splash pad, but then he went off course by turning the car toward a trailer that was set up near the cones. We in the back seat ducked down preparing for impact, but somehow he missed it. When the cruiser came to a stop, three of the four car doors flew open. We all jumped out of the car and landed in the dirt, leaving the driver in the car all by himself.

The most boring time came when our firearms instructor had us sitting in the classroom after lunch and made us watch this video. The video was about cars being shot up, but with different calibers of bullets. We were all drifting in and out of conciseness, because we had to sit there for so long. I noticed that one of my classmates was having a harder time than the rest of us. While I watched him, his eyes would close, his head would drop and then his body would start to lean. Then, he would catch himself, wake up and look around to see if anyone had saw him. Trying to refocus so that he could continue watching the video only lasted a few moments, then the process starting all over again.

I must have watched him for about another ten minutes, before he finally leaned too far, fell out of his seat and crashed to the floor. The instructor thought he had fainted. The classmate was too embarrassed to say otherwise, so the instructor called for medical attention. That call brought a medic to the academy to check him out. While lying on the floor, they put cold towels on his head and the whole bit. He finally assured them that he was okay and that he could continue with class. Now seated again, he looked over at me and we both smiled. A short time after that the instructor gave us a break. As we all fell out into the hallway laughing, we knew he had faked the whole fainting spell. He had been fighting falling asleep, just like the rest of us and only fell out of his chair because that boring video had put him to sleep.

Downtime for us included playing a lot of ping pong in the break room. There was one classmate that beat everyone. As a matter of fact, he had beaten everyone in our class several times and that made the staff bring in a veteran officer to challenge him. They played and the veteran tried his best. Yes, he got his ass kicked too.

It was around week six when our grades, up until that point, were posted. From there, they were posted weekly. The majority of us were passing, but there were a few that were falling behind. One classmate had not passed a single test at that point. He was a good guy, but failing miserably. Collectively, we decided to help him study so that he would not get kicked out of our academy class. We formed study groups and really focused on him to help him pass the upcoming test. He passed that next test with a seventy, but without our continued help, he returned to failing tests immediately. The commander finally talked him into resigning from the class and then offered him a constable's job securing the city's library, and then he was gone. In the weeks to come, others would be leaving before we graduated, as well.

At the academy, we had some kind of written test almost daily. I always finished quick. Leaving the classroom, I would head to our unofficial meeting place, which was where the ping pong table was located. I would sit there and wait for whoever finished next. We would then play ping pong until the whole class had finished. We all would frequently discuss the test and the answers we had given. I routinely tested in the 80-85 range even though I rarely studied. But there was the exception of the emergency medical response exam. With this exam, I nearly failed by only scoring a 69 the first time around. I had to retake the exam the next day and scored a 70 on it.

During the twenty-two weeks of police academy training, we had a host of visitors come from various organizations; The Policeman's Benevolent Association, multiple insurance companies, and other fraternal police organizations as well. Most of them walked away with a payroll deducted sliced from our wages. The last one to come see us was The Bridgeport Guardians. A minority police officer's advocacy group, the guardians watched over racial inequality for its members. When necessary, they had a history of suing the department for racial inequality and more. Winning many of those lawsuits lead to major changes in departments' procedures in the past.

The 9mm Beretta semi-automatic pistol was the department's standard issued gun. After each classmate forked over four hundred and eleven dollars to our firearms instructor, we each were assigned our gun and three fifteen round magazines. This would be the first time I ever touched a gun. Before we were allowed to handle or fire them, we had to take a course and study the gun's nomenclature. We were also taught how to disassemble, clean and re-assemble them. When we were done with all of that, we were cleared to use our guns and to take them home, or so we thought.

For me, I was told that I could not bring my gun home. It seemed that when the department submitted my information for my gun permit, it was rejected. I knew that my younger brother had previously been arrested for some offense and that he had used my name to get out of it. Although I had previously gone to court to have the situation cleared up, the paperwork hadn't made through the state's bureaucracy. Lucky for me, I had kept all the court documents and had anticipated this problem. I had given copies of the documents to the department and the internal affairs commander prior to starting the academy. So,

DAVID DANIELS, III

I was surprised they did not realize they already had the information they needed. Several weeks went by and during that time I would be issued my gun daily, but at the day's end, I would have to give it back to my instructors. After about two weeks of this, I came to class and after inspection the instructor handed me my gun, but this morning something was different. With a smile on his face, he looked at me and whispered.

"Today, you can keep it."

To say that I was truly relieved and happy would be an understatement. I understood that owning a gun is an awesome responsibility and how that responsibility is heightened, if you have children in your home. Children are fascinated by guns and have a natural curiosity about them. When I took my gun home, I removed the magazine and expelled the round from the chamber and made sure it was safe and unloaded. I then called my daughter Joy into the kitchen and told her that Daddy now has a gun.

I let her hold it and touch it. As she did, I explained to her the dangers it held. I talked to her about how much destruction it was capable of. As I watched her curiosity fade, I took the gun back and told her to never go looking for it or to touch it ever again. She looked up at me and simply said okay. I put it inside a locked box, that my wife had brought me for such purposes, and hid it in our bedroom. My daughter, never ever once, talked about guns after that.

Toward the end of the academy, basketball season started and some of the veteran officers asked me if I was going to play with them. I talked to our academy commander about it and he advised me not to play. Fearing that I could be hurt or worse, rendering me unable to complete the academy. The veteran officers told me that it was not against the rules, so I played anyway. During the very second game, I sprained a finger on my right hand and pretty much hid the injury so that I could stay in the academy until completion.

BLACK & BLUE IN BRIDGEPORT

In the waning days of classes, leading up to graduation, things were slowing down and we were allowed time for some social things. We selected our class speaker, planned our graduation party and made our plans for life after the police academy. Although, there was a situation going on with one recruit that we could not ignore.

At about fifteen weeks into our training, detectives from our internal affairs division started making weekly visits to our classroom. During each visit they would remove this one Hispanic female recruit. She would be gone for a few minutes and then return the class and her seat with no words or explanation. It was rumored that her boyfriend was a drug dealer and that might be the reason for the frequent class removals. Some thought she had been placed there just to spy on the rest of us. This is why nobody would get too close to her or share much information with her. She was smart as a whip, always had the top grade on every exam and was doing well. The exception for her came when we had shotgun training. When she fired that weapon, it blew her right off her feet. We would choose her as class spokesman to deliver a speech at our graduation.

The two days before leaving the academy for good, we were let out of the classroom to go to the police supply store for our new uniforms. While there, we were told what platoon individually we would be going into. Then we were shuttled to the department to get issued our badges and to take our police ID pictures. My badge number was 801. As I sat in front of the camera to take my ID photo, I saw my reflection as a police officer for the first time. My mind drifted back to my childhood and I remembered that day us kids were talking with that black police officer in P.T. Barnum. As I was told to 'smile' my reflection changed and there with me now was Officer Lafayette White, smiling back at me. I was the proudest, but also humbled by what I saw in front of me. I felt an exhilaration of spirit that I could never convey in words.

All the pressure was off now. We would be graduating soon and we could feel it. Back at the academy, we had one more surprise still to come and we did not see this one coming. While in class again, in came the internal affairs detectives, yet again to remove that same classmate. After a brief period, the academy commander entered the room and informed us that she would not be returning to class, because she had now been dismissed. We were in shock and did not know what to think. She had arranged our party, she was to be our class speaker at graduation and she had one of highest grade point averages in the class. Now she was gone? We were all speechless for what seemed like an eternity. No one spoke a word and this was my first glimpse into the cold, heartless, homophobic and racist place that I had decided to come to work for. After the bad news, we finished up our coursework somehow and got our notebooks in order to leave for the day.

The next day in class was a blur. A lot of the activity was going on preparing for tomorrow's graduation ceremony at city hall. Since the removal of our classmate, I was then voted by my classmates to deliver the class speech. That meant I had to go home and write a speech on top of getting myself ready for the occasion.

What most people don't realize about becoming a police officer back then is the considerable expenses involved. The initial outlay of funds was great because we had to buy; our own guns, bullets, uniforms, boots, leather gear, hat, jacket, handcuffs and other necessary equipment. The only things the department issued to us were; a rain coat, rubber boots, a bullet proof vest and riot gear. I believe the initial costs were nearly fifteen hundred dollars to acquire all that was needed. Our starting salaries for our first year would be just twenty-three thousand dollars annually. There was also a standing rule that no first year officer could work any overtime. This was especially bad for me because I was making over thirty thousand dollars a year, before I left the telephone company. Taking a pay cut like that with a wife, daughter and a new house was a stressful time for us. On the other hand, none of that mattered because tomorrow morning, I would be realizing my life dream. I was finally becoming a Bridgeport Police Officer.

BLACK & BLUE IN BRIDGEPORT

That night I could not sleep. I tossed and turned thinking about my childhood home and the people there. I also wondered about what kind of police officer I would become. Although my night was pretty much sleepless, I rose early. Showered and shaved, I put on my whole uniform for the first time. I checked my weapon, my leather gear, my buttons, my boots and other necessary implements. I paused to see my reflection in the mirror for good measure and I was pleased by what I saw. Back in our police academy classroom, I looked at all of my classmates and I was proud about how we all became close and had looked out for each other the whole way. Actually, a few got closer than others and had love affairs that left one couple with a baby. Either way, I was happy for everyone and then I went off into the corner to work on my speech.

We stood for inspection for the last time and were issued white gloves to wear during the ceremony. From that point forward, a fluttery of activity commenced. Some classmates got last minute speeches from our instructors. We practiced our group entry. After that, we were all dismissed. With everyone driving their own cars, the last thing to do was to meet at City Hall for the graduation ceremony.

The graduation took place in the Common Council's Chambers. We lined up single file and with military precision walked into chamber right down front and were seated. The hall was not just filled with family, friends, politicians and police personnel, but there were also bright lights everywhere, while television cameras were filming and flashbulbs constantly flashing. At the podium, the Mayor spoke. Police Officials from Shelton and Stratford spoke. The Union President spoke and the Hispanic and Guardians Presidents also spoke.

As the class spokesman, I went up to deliver my speech. I thanked the Academy staff for taking the time and giving us the attention while training us. I told the people assembled that we would try and make them proud. I then sat down. We were individually called to the podium to receive our state certifications and to stand together as a group. Once all of the certificates were passed out, we were asked to raise our right hands and we all took the police officer's oath. Our loved ones were then ushered to the front and given our department badges to pin them upon our uniforms. I chose my mother to do me the honor. After the final congratulation from our commander, the ceremony was officially over.

The families then rained down on us with hugs and kisses and another barrage of pictures were taken as well. We had been instructed early to meet at the steps of City Hall to take a class picture, so we all met up there. After the photo was taken, I raised my hands over my head and clenched my fists in happiness, because I had finally done it.

Right across the street from where we were at City Hall was The Bridgeport Police Headquarters. I, with four other classmates, decided to walk over and introduce ourselves to our new captain. He immediately chastised us for not having our badge and name tag on our outer most garments. He then advised us that we would be off for the next three days, then joining up with the platoon on the 4 p.m.-12 p.m. shift.

That evening we had our class party at a local hotel. We ate, we drank, told stories and laughed at all we had been thru in the academy. The staff partied with us and passed out booby prizes that were relative to our academy experience. That recruit that fell out of his chair during that boring video was given a seat belt. I was given the rope that I used as a belt that day I forgot mine at home. Even though we all had our guns on, we all danced and was having a good time. Then, out of nowhere, that recruit that had been dismissed from the academy, walked in. Everyone paused and went to clamor around her. We hugged and kissed her. We conveyed our sorrow about what had happened to her and she tried to be a trooper about it, but I could see the hurt in her eyes.

As the evening wore on, classmates started leaving the party one by one. I finally left, but headed to New York to celebrate even further and

BLACK & BLUE IN BRIDGEPORT

only to return home in the wee hours of the morning. When I arrived, one of my neighbors had left a copy of the Bridgeport Telegram up against my front door. As I picked it up, I was surprised to see myself on the front page. There I was, in full police uniform with my clenched fists in the air, surrounded by some of my classmates at City Hall. I smiled, entered my home quietly as not to wake my still sleeping wife and daughter.

Chapter V
The Ups, Downs and Joy Stormy Weather

Catching the city bus to go babysit some of my younger cousins wasn't new to me, so I jumped on the bus headed to the east end of Bridgeport. My Aunt Beverly Wade, my cousins and her three small children were living in a new development called New Era Court, just off Stratford Avenue down Central Avenue. Since I was a teenager now, my aunt often asked me to watch the children while she ran some errands.

After getting off the bus and walking through the development's courtyard, I notice three girls standing around talking. All of them were about my age and one of them was Nina, who I knew from previous visits to my aunt's house. Nina saw me walking and calls me over to where they all are talking. Nina introduces me to the other two young ladies and we strike up light conversation.

One of the girls I meet is named Toni and she has red hair and freckles. During our group conversation, I find that I am very interested in Toni, her conversation and the looks we give each other, back and forth. When our group conversation ends and I am walking away, I dawn a big smile at the fact that I not only enjoyed the conversation, but I also left with Toni's telephone number. I called her that night, Toni and I spoke for hours. I told her she was the prettiest girl I had

BLACK & BLUE IN BRIDGEPORT

ever seen. We made plans to see each other again on that next Saturday at the carnival.

Saturday came quick. I unbraid my afro, put on some cheap cologne and head for the park. The Midway is a small traveling carnival that came to Bridgeport every summer around the fourth of July. They would setup the small rides, games and vendors in the same area of the park and hundreds of people would visit the carnival over the next few weeks. Shortly after I get to the park, I see Toni as she's walking toward me and she wasn't alone. Toni introduces me to her friend Libby and her boyfriend Terry. Although I did not know she was bringing her friends, it didn't matter, I was still happy to just see Toni again.

Now, all assembled, we begin strolling around the carnival grounds holding hands, exchanging glances and big smiles. People were everywhere. They were eating, playing games of chance and getting on rides as carnival music was blaring all around us on this beautiful sunny day. As we walk, I see a lot of people from my hood and they see me as well. Looking that them and then Toni, I was so proud to be walking with such a pretty girl.

All of the sudden, out of nowhere, the sky seemed to open up and began showering us with rain. In a panic, we all run in different directions seeking shelter. As I wait for the rain to clear, I realize Toni isn't with me and I am alone in my hiding spot. After the shower passes, I go looking for her. I see them off in the distance. But as I continue to look, I also see another kid with them. Another boy is walking with them, next to Toni, in my place. I stop in my tracks and stare for a moment as the hurt and embarrassed set in. What were they doing? I didn't understand what was happening, but even at fifteen years old, I knew it was best not to go and catch up to them. Instead, I left the park before they saw me and made a vow to myself to never call her again.

Later that summer, I met another young lady. Liz was pretty, petite and Latin. She quickly became my official girlfriend. We fell in love and my thoughts about Toni faded. Although I would see Toni in the city from time to time, we never really spoke again. Right after I graduated high school, I took a job working at ATI, which was an aerosol plant in the neighboring city of Milford. Working hard in that factory and having little to show for it made me seriously consider going to college. As the fall season came in, my grandmother had a heart attack. During her hospitalization, we were told that she needed heart by-pass surgery, so I visited with her daily. On one of my visits, while walking toward her room, I hear a familiar voice speak out to me.

"Hi. David."

I turn around to see Toni standing there in a nurse's uniform.

"Hello, Toni."

"What are you doing in the hospital?"

I tell her about my grandmother. At the time, she was a senior in high school working at the hospital as a dietary aid. We talk for awhile. I tell her I have decided to go to college and will be heading to Norfolk State University in September. I shared that my relationship with Liz had fizzled out months before and she admitted that she was just coming out of a relationship as well. After a little more conversation, she gives me her telephone number and I tell her that I will call. Later that night I called and we discussed the park incident. She explained that the boy I saw with them was Terry's friend and that she had no interest in him. She admits how wondering for so long about why I disappeared after the rain, had made her sad. We talked about our new found relationship freedom and I remembered how easy it was to talk to her all over again. From there, we spoke at least once, just about every week. A short time later, Miriam, who was Reggie's girlfriend and Toni's classmate, tells me that Toni wants to take me to her prom. The very next time I speak with Toni, I agree to take her. Our weekly talks became daily ones that quickly lead to visits. I meet her family and I bring her to P.T. to meet mine.

By the time the proms rolls around, not only are we inseparable, we are in love and I get scared. We both knew that I would be leaving in September to go away to college. Falling in love with Toni made me want to always be next to her and that was the exact opposite of my plans. I wasn't a fan of the idea of a long distance love affair. I figured the distance would surely kill the relationship. By the end of the summer, just as I had feared, I didn't want to leave her. We talked about it and agreed not to cheat on one another. She came along when my Father dropped me at the bus station to go away to Norfolk. We wrote each other every week. Her letters made me miss home and miss her more. She told me about my sister being pregnant, about my mother losing weight and all I could do was look forward to the Thanksgiving break. It would be my first time, returning home from college.

After those first few months and a twelve hour Greyhound bus ride, I finally made it home for Thanksgiving. At home, I saw my mother, my brothers and sisters and told them all about my college experiences. I enjoyed sharing my stories, but it wasn't long before I left again, heading for the east end to see Toni. Reuniting with her for that little bit of time made me whole again. After the holiday, I returned to school only thinking about my next visit home.

Around that time, Toni decided to join her friend Libby by attending Bennett College in Greensboro, North Carolina. This excited me because now we would only be one state away from each other. The first time I went to visit her was by my trusted means of travel, the Greyhound bus. After an eight hour ride, I quickly found out that she didn't like Bennett College or North Carolina. This made it no surprise when she soon returned to the Northeast to go to school in New York. She started working at The European Bank and attended Pace University. Throughout all the moving around and the long distance, we managed to stay together.

In 1978, we had already decided that we were going to get married, but to my surprise, Toni lovingly shared with me that I was going to be a father. On April 17, 1979, Joy Carolyn Daniels was born. I was right there, in the delivery room, watching her being born. Without a doubt, this is one of my greatest life experiences. I was so moved by her birth that I cried that night. Wondering if I could take care of her and what type of father would I be. With Joy in a walker and our families in attendance, November 3, 1979 marks the day that Toni and I became husband and wife. It was a simple ceremony on another sunny day briefly visited by a passing shower. Toni in her royal blue dress and me in my winter white double breasted suit, looking like we just stepped out of Ebony Magazine.

The Gary Crooks Community Center is where our reception was held with our guests of about one hundred and fifty or so. We all danced and ate soul food that my mother and aunts had prepared and Toni's Aunt Ada, she brought all the liquor. Unfortunately, we never went on a honeymoon. Money was tight, but we were thankful for our families and friends. They are the ones who chipped in to give us the reception by cooking all the food and buying all the drinks for our guests, while my friend Keith Williams, DJ'ed the night away. Our first place together was staying on the top floor of Toni's aunt's house.

I was only twenty-three years old then. Those first few years were tough and I didn't have a clue as to how to conduct myself. Knowing that my parents separated when I was nine or ten years old, I had no clear idea of what a successful married life looked like. I didn't like sitting at home and found it hard to stop running the streets with my boys. Toni, on the other hand, continued to go to school, got a job at City Trust Bank that advanced her career in banking, while continuing to take really good care of me and Joy. We argued quite a bit because I was still so immature and Toni was only asking that I be more responsible. I wasn't saving money, wasn't pursuing any goals and over time that lead to us separating a few times and sadly, I had a few affairs.

Thankfully, I finally got with the program, start working together with Toni and our efforts lead to the purchase of our first house. It was a newly constructed duplex style house, down a dead-end street on the city's north end. Just two streets over from an elementary school, we knew that Joy would have plenty of children to play with. Additionally, I knew some of our neighbors on the street as well and that made for hopes of an ideal living situation for us.

Then real life happens. Toni and I both came to learn that there is a big difference between renting and owning. The cost of maintaining the house was major. The mortgage, taxes and insurance costs added up quickly and we had to swing about thirteen hundred a month, just to stay in our home. This didn't include utilities, clothing or even food. It was a brand new experience for us and it was an adjustment, but it wasn't as bad as it was going to get.

When the time came for me to leave the telephone company, my income took a dramatic drop to start as a new police officer. Making it worse, the rule that new officers are not allowed to work any overtime hours their first year, hurt my prospects to supplement that lost income. This put the pressure right back on us and by the time I graduated from the police academy, my marriage was on shaky legs.

Being on the job as a police officer has its dangers, but there are other dangers that I didn't take into account that also made a big impact on our life. After being involved in my third motor vehicle accident on the job, I sustained neck and shoulder injuries, two broken fingers, a three inch cut on the back of my head and other scrapes and bruises. More importantly, these injuries lead to some memory loss and frequent headaches. Just a month before that accident, I had totaled my 1987 Chevy Camaro in another serious crash and didn't have a personal car. Coming home from the hospital and being stuck at home led me to finding out that Toni had been reading a book about divorce. Things were already looking bad and now I had to add finding a new place to stay to the list. This was another spin on the downward spiral my life was in at the time.

When the New Year came around, I was doing much better physically, but my marriage was still suffering. Toni and I still weren't getting along, so it seemed better for us to separate, yet again. I brought a brand new 1990 Camaro, a bedroom set and moved to an apartment in the town of West Haven, about a twenty minute drive from Bridgeport. During my first few weeks in the new apartment, Toni and I continued to argue daily. It seemed as if we were two different people from the two who had been through so much together. Our relationship, that spanned ten years, was now over and we both had to find a better way to accept that.

With all the changes going on at home, it all seemed like my life had been turned upside down. Returning to work was no different. I was out of work for about a month, only to return to a very different police department. Prior to my accident, our department utilized a platoon system to manage personnel. This system allowed for officers to swing the clock and work on a rotation system to a new shift each week. When I came back, we were now on squad rotations with fixed shifts and officers were placed according to seniority. This ushered in; new car assignments, getting used to new people, working in new areas of the city and new supervisors. This made the burnout factor go high and officer's morale went low.

Our latest contract, negotiated every two years between The City and the Police Union, had gone to binding arbitration. This meant no agreement had been reached on working conditions, benefits, staffing levels, wages, safety and other matters to govern the Police services that we would be rendering to the city itself. Adding to the madness, a court decision on the recent sergeant's test had racial tensions at a heightened level and an unexpected transition in leadership was about to make all matters worse.

Chapter VI
Year of the Rookie
How The Game Is Played

When I returned home from college, I only lived with my mother for a few months. I spent most of that time working and hanging out with my girlfriend on the east end in Bridgeport. I got married to my first wife Olivia, moved out and it was only a few years before I joined the police department to complete the academy. Damn near right out of the academy, I was assigned to a patrol car that covered P.T. Barnum.

The drug called crack had hit the projects hard and I quickly noticed that these kids were a different breed of drug dealer. Unlike back in my day, when dealers tried to hide and stay away from trouble, these new dealers were flashy and violent. They would deal their drugs right out in the open and run right up to cars to make sells. Even the crack-head addicts would walk right into the projects in plain view and buy drugs. When I left to go away to college, all the dealers were older and they conducted business in the building's hallways. If not there, they sold out of someone's apartment and never would they sell to kids. But these kids would sell to anyone, including kids and on slow days, they would beat up some of the crack-heads to amuse themselves. They also moved in groups and they were operating under some kind of understand together, between the all the buildings.

DAVID DANIELS, III

While on patrol, I was surprised to discover that one of my friend's younger brothers and nephews were selling drugs in the projects around building seventeen. Growing up and going to school with their parents, a lot of the kids were just babies back then, but now they were controlling the drug trade out there. Across the drive, building one was controlled by another family that I knew and close by in building two, there were yet another group of kids that I had watched grow up from diapers. I knew them all and they knew me. Most of them gave me respect as a man and a police officer and would move along, if I came anywhere near them.

My friend's nephews had a bad rep out there and there were whispers about murders they had committed and beatings they had dished out to people. A lot of folks were shook in regards to them. On one occasion, I walked into the courtyard between buildings twelve and thirteen and they stared me down. Refusing to leave the area, one of them got salty with me. I looked him up and down and said.

"Hold up. I grew up out here, so I know how the game is played."

I got on my radio and called for a couple of adjoining patrol cars. Once assembled, I asked the officers to help me search the three or four abandoned cars parked at the location. Within ten minutes, we came up with several bundles of drugs they had stashed inside them. I turned to look at the salty one with a smile on my face.

"Looks like it's time for ya'll to re-up."

I laughed and we left the project and went back to headquarters to tag up all the contraband we had discovered.

The next shift that came up for me to patrol P.T. was on a Sunday. I stopped downtown at the news corner and got a Bridgeport Post Sunday Edition newspaper to bring along. I then drove to P.T. and pulled up right between buildings seventeen and sixteen, where they operated. As I was driving up, they all looked, frowned and began to leave the area. I smiled and told them to have a great day. I then sat on the hood of the patrol car and proceeded to read the paper. In a few minutes I got called on the police radio. I answered up and was told to call headquarters. I did and was told to move my patrol car out of there right now.

The DEA, the FBI, the statewide narcotics taskforce and my old classmate, Ron Bailey were doing surveillances in that area and I had run everybody off. I was quick to realize two things; the first was that P.T. Barnum was hotter than I could ever have imagined and second, that in police work the left hand hardly ever knew what the right hand was doing. This came as a valuable life lesson that would serve me positively over the course of my career.

Within a time frame of two to three years all of those kids, dozens of them, were all charged, arrested, indicted, tried, convicted and sentenced. Some of them got just a few years and got out, but most got lengthy prison terms. I'm talking fifteen to twenty year bids. Another few of them are still in there to this day and may never ever get out, while others died in prison. In the bigger picture of things, when the old leave or are taken away, a new crop of dealers are always there to step right up to take their places.

About a week had passed before I got called out of P.T. I was sent to patrol the area around Marina Village, which is another city housing project on the south end of the city, when a young lady flagged me down. I pulled over to the curbside and she walked up to the driver side window peered in. She then asked me something.

"Are you Officer Daniels?"

"Yes, I am. Why?"

"Are you guys looking for Frank Nitti?"

Frank Nitti was not his real name, but I knew who she was speaking of. He was a cousin to one of the drug dealing families out in P.T., but his specialty was ripping off the other dealers operating in the projects. He could have easily been a model for the character "Omar" on the television series The Wire. Just like that character, people were scared of Frank Nitti as well. It was rumored that his last attempt to rob a dealer ended with him getting shot. After that situation, nobody had seen him for a couple of days.

"Yes, we are looking for him, why?"

With a scared look on her face, she quickly responded.

"He's in my apartment in very bad shape and needs medical attention."

I put up my hand to tell her to hold on as I called into headquarters and requested a Sergeant. Minutes later, a black Sergeant arrived along with two additional patrol cars. She then told me where she lived.

"Do you know if he is armed?"

"No, he's not."

"Okay. Now I need you to go home, unlock the door and then leave."

While she was doing that we decided to have an ambulance come silently to the area and park up the block. Once they were on site, the Sergeant told the other two officers to go to the back door of the residence. I went in the front door first, with the Sergeant trailing behind me. I crept to the back door and unlocked it so the two other officers could gain entry.

We all gathered and slowly proceeded up the stairs, then into the master bedroom. There he was all laid out on the bed and too weak to fight or even try to run. I looked down at him.

"Frank you ready to get out of here?"

He looked and just smiled at me. The Sergeant called for the ambulance to roll up. Frank had been shot a few days prior, but fearful of getting arrested on the spot, he would not go to the hospital. I lifted him out of the bed. We brought him downstairs where he was put on a gurney, removed from that apartment and I would never see him again.

The black Sergeant turned to me and said.

"Good job. I'm going to write this up and put you in for a commendation."

BLACK & BLUE IN BRIDGEPORT

I thought wow to myself and that would be pretty cool. It did not take long before I realized that black officers on the force hardly ever received commendations for anything and that included me, because I never did either. Later in my career I got close. I was included on a group commendation, but never as an individual. Not for anything I did in the past, the present or the future.

Chapter VII
Uncivilized Brutality
You See and Don't See

For the first few months on the job, I just tried to fit in a well as I could. The car I was assigned to patrolled the north end of the city. I loved the job so much, at the end of my shifts I didn't even want to go home. I could not play basketball anymore, because my sprained finger was still healing. I found time to attend a few games anyway, to support the guys. Midway through the season I rejoined the team, but was soon kicked off after disagreeing with the coach, whom I believe was an acting Sergeant at the time. I could have fought to stay on the team, but I couldn't make him play me, so I let it roll.

For the next twelve weeks I would be in the Field Training Officer (FTO) Program. To complete the program, I needed to ride with a different training officer each week. Each officer I rode with let me do certain things, but driving the squad car was not included. They would document my performance and then report to my supervisors. I had to write the reports, handle disputes, issue tickets and basically listen to them and learn. At the end of that period, I had no deficiencies and was assigned my own vehicle to use for patrol.

That first few weeks were surreal and I seem to only get calls for service to deal with people that I knew. One guy that I knew had beaten up his sister because he wanted her to stay home and take

BLACK & BLUE IN BRIDGEPORT

care of her child. I had played ball with him several times over the years, but his mother had called the police, so I had to arrest dude even though I didn't want to. Another call sent me to intervene in a dispute over a stolen moped. Once I arrived, I knew both parties. Yet another call took me to a home where a guy, believing that his girlfriend was cheating on him, returned home from work unexpected. He then caught her in the act with her suitor and beat her up. I knew him and had to arrest him also. Then I had to call his job in Stamford to come pick up the company truck. I felt bad for him about all that was happening to him. Another call brought me home to P.T. where I was greeted by a woman. I had grown up around her and she was explaining to me how someone fighting with her granddaughter had slashed face with a straight razor, just minutes before my arrival. Throughout all my calls, I maintained my objectivity and handled the situations as best I could, although they were strenuous situations.

February the 15th started out as a routine work day. I reported to headquarters, stood in front of my locker to change into uniform, grabbed my summons book along with other necessities and walked out into the dayroom to stand in line-up. During line-up, we are advised of past and present hazards or activities on our post. We are also updated on what cars had been stolen that day and given our car assignment then sent off into night. When we leave headquarters to begin our shift, we would activate our radios then call base, using a code, to advise dispatch that your car was now in service and ready to receive calls on your assigned post. My patrol car was Amber 26. After receiving confirmation, I headed to the north end of town.

After about an hour into my shift, I realized that I had not received another transmission over the radio, since I activate it. It had just started to drizzle with rain, so I thought that my car radio may have been malfunctioning. I stopped at a payphone and called the dispatcher to advise them of this condition. I explained that my handset seemed to be okay and that I would continue patrolling my post. As I was heading north on Main Street the radio broke its silence in my patrol car.

"Amber 26"

I grabbed the microphone.

"Amber 26 on."

"Return to HQ per S1"

"10-4."

I quickly turned my patrol car in the right direction and headed back to headquarters for further instruction. Once at police headquarters, I was advised by a sandy haired acting Sergeant that I had missed a call for service. I informed him of my last call to the dispatcher, where I explained that I was not receiving any calls on the car radio and that I believed it had been intermittently malfunctioning. Once I told him that, he let me know that there were no other cars available for me to drive and that I could not go back out in that car. I was then told that my car assignment was terminated, because he was grounding my car. I also needed to go get my rain gear because my new assignment was walking downtown in the rain for a few hours. After that, I would be partnered up with another veteran officer until the shift ended.

I went to my locker, put on my rain gear and headed out on foot down the hill toward Main Street. At the corner of Main, I turned to walk south into the downtown area. As I walked, I stopped at businesses along the way and went inside to introduce myself. I saw a familiar face as I was passing in front of the Hilton Hotel. I crossed the street and that person asked if I was still playing ball. I told him that I hadn't been playing lately because I was too busy. As we stood there having our conversation, my police radio transmitted the code that let me know an officer needed assistance. As I was now listening harder, his location was Bridgeport's Train Station. The station was right up the street and around the corner from where I was standing. I excused myself and ran all the way to the train station.

BLACK & BLUE IN BRIDGEPORT

With no other patrol cars out front, I was the first to arrive. I ran up the stairs, entered the doorway to the main lobby and looked around. In the distance, I saw a veteran officer calmly standing partially in an office doorway straight ahead. I thought to myself, what's going on here? What was the emergency? I calmly walked in the direction toward the officer and once I got there, I peered into the office. There I saw two young black men in handcuffs. From first glance, they both appeared intoxicated to me. As they were looking at the doorway, they both recognized me and quickly started walking toward me and the door, as they professed their innocence. I cut them off in mid-sentence and ushered them back into the room.

As I stepped back to the doorway, without a break to breathe, they continued their story by telling me that they hadn't snatched anybody's purse. Next, they started cursing at the arresting officer. Before I could say my next word, another veteran Italian Officer pushed by and entered the room. Without asking a question, he started screaming at them about addressing police officers as punks or motherfuckers as he continued to walk right up into their faces. He then reached out, grabbed the taller handcuffed suspect and yanked him close to himself. Holding him there for a brief second, the Officer then proceeded to throw him over a table that was in the room. The shorter suspect, who was also handcuffed, leaned over to look at his partner on the floor and the same Officer punched him in the face, twice.

All this started and happened in seconds and I was numb. Standing there, I was in shock. I could not believe what I had just witnessed. As a reflex, I pushed the door open more. Figuring if the brutality Officer knew that other people could see what he was doing, he would stop. Instead, he attempted to kick the suspect that he had thrown over the table, but his feet got tangled up and he nearly fell. The suspect then yelled out to me.

"Dave! You gonna let this happen?"

Somehow, his words shocked me back into reality. I quickly stepped into the room, reached down and picked him up off the floor.

"I got you."

With my arm wrapped around his, I proceeded to walk him out of the office and past at least thirty-five other Officers. As we were walking, I was telling him that it was over. As we stepped through the same doorway into the lobby, another veteran Officer spoke directly to me as we passed.

"You should have closed that fucking door!"

I just looked at him and continued to walk toward the exit, because following us was the brutality Officer and he was still screaming at the top of his lungs.

I walked the suspect down the stairs, outside and toward a police car waiting at the curbside when he started to buckle. He then tells me that the handcuffs were too tight. I looked down at his wrist and I could see a trickle of blood where the cuffs had cut into his skin. He pleaded with me to loosen them and tried to convince me.

"I won't run."

As I reached for my keys to adjust his handcuffs, another Officer speaks up.

"If you loosen those cuffs, you're not putting him in my car."

I reach down and adjust the handcuffs and then double lock them, so they could not get any tighter. Then the Officer jumps into the curbside cruiser and speeds away, leaving us both standing there clueless.

Another patrol car pulled up to us and I quickly put the suspect in the rear seat. I hopped in the front passenger seat to accompany him on the ride to booking. As we rode, from the back seat the prisoner had a lot to say.

"He only did that to us because we were black, that punk motherfucker. If I didn't have these handcuffs on, I would have kicked his ass. You know that shit wasn't right. I'm going to complain."

BLACK & BLUE IN BRIDGEPORT

As I sat there silently, I heard him, but I was still trying to sort out what I had just experienced for myself. Shortly after we arrived at booking, the second suspect was brought in by a female Officer, who quickly disappeared into the night. Now both suspects reunited, they again began to exclaim their innocence and talk about what had happened to them at the train station. Eventually, they were processed and put into holding cells.

I went downstairs, because it was now nine o'clock. It was about time for me to hook-up with the Officer I would be riding with the rest of my shift. I went into the locker room to stow my raingear and in a fit of rage and frustration, I punched and kicked my locker instead. With all the noise I was making, before anyone could see that it was me, I went out into the parking lot. I found the veteran Officer waiting for me in a patrol car outside and as soon as I got into the car, he speaks his first words to me.

"You know Dave, on this job you see things and you don't see things."

I just looked over at him and decided right then that I would be completely silent for the rest of our shift.

At midnight, we finished the shift and I headed home. Although I was happy to get home, that night I could not sleep. Whenever it was that I finally fell asleep, I abruptly woke up in a cold sweat and sat on the edge of my bed. My mind was forcing me, frame by frame to revisit the train station incident over and over again. My mind then repeated played every incident of police brutality that I had seen from my childhood to manhood. My stomach was in knots and I felt like such a failure for not doing more to stop it faster than I did. After a while and with tears in my eyes, I unknowingly drifted back to sleep.

Around noon the next day, I got out of bed and started thinking about this new situation I was now part of and how it did not fit in with me already trying to stay low key. It had only been a few weeks since my return to work after been in an on-the-job car accident that rumors were saying I was going to be found at fault and facing discipline. I was working for a Captain that everyone hated and no one trusted. It was hard for everyone working under a bunch of acting Sergeants that were all bitter over being stuck in that acting capacity. The Bridgeport Guardian organization had sued the city and police departments in federal court over the testing procedure and put everything on hold. Even a few of the Sergeants had been disciplined by the courts for civil rights violations. There was so much going on, so I needed to find some time to go and talk to Ted Meekins about what had occurred the night before at the train station. He was the current President of The Bridgeport Guardians and I hoped he would be able to give me some guidance.

As usual, I arrived at Police Headquarters about 3:30 p.m. to get ready for my shift. I stood in line-up and was beside myself to hear that my assignment was changed from patrol to sitting at the front desk. This assignment was unusual because sitting at the front desk for the sick, lame, lazy or in trouble. This was my first clue that things were really going wrong. Either way, I went upstairs to the front desk and sat there waiting to see what would happen next.

About an hour later, a Sergeant came upstairs and looked at me with a smirk on his face as he happily tells me.

"The Captain wants to see you downstairs in his office."

I got up and made my way downstairs to the Captains office. Once there, I knocked on the door and was told to enter. The Captain motioned for me to close the door and to have a seat. Now seated in front of the Captain's desk, he looked over at me.

"I hear you're upset about something that occurred at the bus station last night?"

I quickly reply hoping he corrected himself.

"The bus station Sir?"

"I mean the train station."

BLACK & BLUE IN BRIDGEPORT

Okay. So he does know about the train station incident, but what did he know and how did he come to know about it? My thoughts began to race through my mind like a car speeding downhill with no brakes. How did he come to ask me about it? Why me? I hadn't said anything to anyone yet. I quickly decided right at that moment, that I was not going to lie about anything.

"Yes, I am upset about what I seen transpire last night at the train station. I saw a veteran Officer man-handle and abuse two handcuffed suspects."

The Captain's eyes opened wide. His face went beet red and it seemed like sweat instantly started forming on his nearly bald head. I could also feel it getting hot in the office, but I moved forward and told him all the details of the incident from beginning to end. At my end, he immediately picked up the phone and called the office of internal affairs. Listening to him on the phone made my heart sank as he repeated everything I had said, word for word to someone on the other end of the line. When he completed his call, he looked over at me and things got crazy.

"We are going to Internal Affairs and you will have to give them a statement."

Without another thought, I knew I did not want this or anything to happen to make the situation worse.

"I don't want to go anywhere or give any statements!"

"I'm not asking you, I'm ordering you to, it's your job."

I sat there totally numb inside. When I dreamed of becoming a police officer, I never imagined being in this position. With all the accidents, my crumbling marriage and now this, I knew my life was getting ready to change yet again and forever.

I do not even remember how I got to the Office of Internal Affairs. Their building was off-site and across town away from the police department. It was all happening so fast and I knew that I could not stop it. I signed the visitors log then was placed into this small office.

DAVID DANIELS, III

I gave my statement and it was recorded. I was shown photos of the whole police force. It was made clear that they wanted a detailed account of what happened, who was there, what was said, everything. I told them everything that I could remember. It seemed like I was there for hours. My testimony implicated three veteran Officers; the one who had committed the brutality, the arresting Officer and the Officer that told me that I should have closed the door to hide what had happened.

The department was in a buzz. Now there were other officers being called into Internal Affairs to give their statements and people moving around everywhere, coming in and out. They took me to another office, off the beaten path, as to hide me from the officers coming in. They all had to sign the same log book, which I signed when I came in, so it really didn't matter. Plus, the Sergeant that came upstairs at headquarters to get me from the front desk was making it a point to bring people by the office I was now sitting in, so that they could see me there.

When I finally got home, I was emotionally drained, bewildered and depressed. I didn't know who to turn to or who to trust. I had been told by internal affairs not to discuss the situation with no one. My whole world was unraveling like a ball of string. My life was falling apart like a house of cards. That night, in my solitude, I felt like a lost child who needed to be held. I just needed someone to tell that things were going to be okay. But I was grown now and had separated from my wife and daughter, so I was alone. I even thought my wife may even like this happening to me. We were still arguing a lot and I thought she hated me. It was another sleepless night.

The next day, I went to visit my daughter and my wife was there. I wanted to tell my wife that I was in trouble. I tried to find the words, but I could not. At some point she looked at me and said.

"I heard you're having problems on the job?"

BLACK & BLUE IN BRIDGEPORT

Fear from that same feeling that maybe she would enjoy hearing that I was, on the job she never wanted me to take, made me just brush her question off.

"You should know me better than that."

I stayed a little while longer, then left to go to work.

When I arrived at police headquarters, expecting to work my regular shift, I was quickly advised that I had been placed on suspension. My suspension was based on pending charges involving the incident at the train station. I could not convey in words what that felt like. I was then taken to Internal Affairs. They wanted more detail of everything, all over again. Again, there were more pictures, more taped recordings and more activity like that which I had experienced the night before. The Internal Affairs Detective told me that I was suspended, along with the others, so I would not be the object of attention, go figure. Back at headquarters, I was told I still had to come to work every day only to be temporarily assigned to the front desk.

The next day the story of the brutality hit the newspapers, clearly naming me and the others as being suspended. I could feel the tension and stares from my co-workers as I made my way through the building on my way to the front desk. People and Officers alike, were turning their backs to me and not speaking too me at all. I left work that night at shifts end in my brand new Chevy Camaro with its windshield covered in spit.

In the coming weeks more spit and turned backs, followed by the dents and scratches showing up on my car. I was a bundle of raw nerves. It was hard for me to come to work, deal with everyone acting like they were and have to worry about my car. I started parking on the street instead of the parking lot, but that didn't do any good. I started documenting the vandalism and because of the public outcry, I was given the Chief's parking spot inside the locked police garage.

I was taken off suspension, only to then be put on administrative notice. This meant that I had to face charges in the train station incident. From there, I was allowed to resume patrol duties, but I quickly found out that no officer would ride with me or back me up on calls. When I would return to headquarters at shifts end and attempt to turn in my paperwork, this particular Sergeant would scrutinize my paperwork. He would make me correct everything to his satisfaction, on the spot, before he would give me the keys to the police garage to retrieve my car. Normal practice was to just turn in our paperwork and it would be handed back to you the next day, if anything needed correcting. At the time, I hated what that Sergeant was doing to me, but it made me a better writer over time, so thanks for that. When I was dispatched, that same Sergeant would get to the location before me and then leave, without saying one word to me. The other Sergeants followed suit and were really riding me hard, calling me out on everything little thing that they could. Again, it was tough, but it all made me a better officer even though I know that was not their intent.

    During this time I was transferred to three different squads. I would arrive at work only to be told that I had been transferred again. During one stretch I was off for eleven days straight with all the transferring. If my voice was recognized on the police radio, my broadcasts were jammed so I couldn't get through to base. I received no back up on calls. If I found myself in a dangerous situation, I was on my own because no officer would back me up and I was driving a solo car, with no partner.

    After a few weeks of all this messy stuff going on, the Captain called me into his office and suggested I get a partner. I was transferred again. This time it was to the red sector of the city on Bridgeport's East End with one of my classmates, Officer Jerry Platt. Our area post started at the beginning of Stratford Avenue, down to the Stratford city line and continued up toward the Bridgeport Hospital area. This section of town was mostly of a minority population. There were a high number of calls for service during a shift, because the area was densely populated. This added to the enhanced criminal activities from; gangs, drug dealing, bars, cleaners, neighborhood stores, several churches and even schools. It was a hot-bed of activity 24-7.

I had met Jerry in the police academy. He was southern, a little older than me and his wife was a veteran Officer. At first, we didn't hit it off too good. He was too gung-ho for me. I was just the opposite, just trying to stay low key. After what I'd been through, I wasn't gung-ho at all. After the first week, Jerry didn't want to ride with me anymore. We had a long talk and decided to give things another try. By this time the train station incident had become daily newspaper coverage. Everyone inside and outside the department was talking about it. It was taking a toll on the both of us. Jerry helped me side-step some of the things the Sergeants were trying to pull on me. He told me that he didn't agree with the way I was being treated.

By the third week of us riding together, a Connecticut Post Reporter wanted to ride with us and interview me about all the harassment stories that were beginning to emerge. He signed a waiver and was given the back seat of our police car for the tour. At first I was reluctant to do the interview, I just wanted it all to go away, but after hearing that the Sergeant that had been riding me for weeks was against it, I agreed to do it. Jon Heller was the reporter. As he rode with us interviewing me, he saw the people in the community coming up to the police car to shake my hand and encourage me as we traveled the east end. We talked about everything that I had experienced. When he asked Jerry how he felt about what was happening to me Jerry quickly replied with 'No Comment.' That made me a bit sad. Previously, in private, Jerry had expressed his opinion and understood my actions. I expected him to speak up to the reporter, but he let me down. Now, I felt alone again. The Mayor, Police Chief and other working supervisors were supposed to be monitoring my calls and the situation. We were to receive only non-threatening calls during that period. Other cars in the sector were expected to give us cover, if there were any dangerous calls.

My last night on the streets, Jerry and I were sent to three 'shots fired' calls back to back. The last one took us to a bodega near East Main Street. There we discovered a young Hispanic male that had been shot and now lying in a pool of blood in the rear of the store. Someone in the store said that the shooter had just left and was running up the street. Jerry instantly jumped in the car, took off in search of the shooter and left me alone in the store with the victim. A crowd started to form. I tried to utilize the radio to convey my condition, but my transmissions were being blocked by other officers. Someone called for an ambulance by telephone and as it arrived, so did a Captain and a Lieutenant. They were my cover on this call, because no other car from that sector came to that location during the incident. After my shift, I finally got a chance to speak to Ted Meekins of the Guardians. After much discussion, I decided to request a transfer off the street. The very next night, the Police Commissioners granted my request to be placed somewhere in the department that I could work with children;

I was then transferred to the Community Services Division. At that time, the office was run by Sergeant Hector Torres. He would make it all the way up the ladder to become Acting Police Chief before finally retiring from the department. Two other Officers; A.J. Perez and Bob Koskuba were also assigned to the division teaching the DARE Program in Bridgeport Public and Parochial Schools. They also did presentations and security surveys for city residents and businesses for the department. We had a little office on the second floor of the old police academy that we shared with the Board of Education Crossing Guards.

My first week there I was a little uncomfortable. With all the things going on around me and all that I was going through, I wasn't sure how I was going to be treated. But to my surprise, they spoke to me, asked me questions and we worked well together. They treated me like one of them, taught me a lot and exposed me to a more positive side of police work that involved community interaction. During this period someone had written threats to me on the police department's elevator door. Evidence of the writings had been sent to the FBI crime lab for analysis and in the coming weeks, a suspect would be named for the threats and the damage to my car, but no one was ever charged.

Later that week, I was again called into Internal Affairs. This time to talk to an FBI agent assigned to this area. He advised me that he had been sending the newspaper articles about the incident and the harassment to Washington. This also included the Justice Department monitoring the case and was considering bringing federal charges against the Officer whom had committed the brutality. I was again interviewed for a couple of hours and then sent home.

During those early days in Community Services, I followed Bob and A.J to their schools to see them work. They taught, did presentations and interacted with the public and I was impressed. D.A.R.E. means Drug Abuse Resistance Education. It's an anti-drug program that is taught to the 5th grade population of The Bridgeport School System. That's about two-thousand children a year. The curriculum components build upon one another. The introduction talks about rights then self-esteem, consequences, risk taking and assertiveness. It has a role modeling component that talks about gang activity and conflict resolution skills also. Taught by a uniformed police officer, this program was the brainchild of the Los Angeles Unified School District and The L.A.P.D. in 1982 and has been taught all over these United States, on military bases and Indian reservations as well.

During that first month in Community Services, the brutality Officer from the train station was brought up on departmental charges. At his inquest, I was the star witness. Not wanting to wait on a decision in his case to be rendered, he chose to retire the next day to save his pension. Sadly, as a response to his retirement, all departmental charges against him were simply dropped. Shortly after that I was sent to Meriden, Connecticut to DARE Officer training from The Connecticut State Police. The two weeks of training were long and grueling. Police Officers were there from cities all over the state; North Stonington, Madison and Norwalk, to name a few. After the first week I wanted to quit, but I pushed through because I wanted to get the opportunity to teach the program to Bridgeport kids. I started liking that idea, so I applied myself while still trying to stay low key. I did not want anyone to figure out who I was in light of the articles that were appearing weekly in the newspapers now. For a few days, I was good and everybody was treating me well. I did not like being gone for the two weeks, because I was now living with my girlfriend Yvette and I had to leave her alone.

Two weeks later, I took my first trip to the west coast to attend the national DARE Conference in Phoenix Arizona. I wasn't quite ready for all that heat. The city was experiencing higher than normal humidity at the time. I was amazed at how flat and brown the city was. You could clearly see for miles, right into the mountains. I saw cactus and palm trees and even Indians. I had a great time along with about fifteen-hundred other police Officers from all over the country. For the opening session, we all attended in full uniform. Seeing that many Officers, all dressed for the job, was as an awesome sight and I was proud to be a part of it all.

We were out in Arizona for a week. We attended seminars and workshops during the day and shopped, dined and sight saw during the evening. During the summer, back home in Bridgeport, I was the subject of more newspaper articles. Preachers were making me the subject of their sermons, people were encouraging me, but my fellow officers were still not speaking to me and turning their backs as I passed them by. My phone rang constantly. Either with reporters wanting to talk, people cussing me out or just hearing silence on the other end. By now, the two Officers named for participating in the brutality, had their hearings and were simply cleared of any wrong doing. I was not called to testify at either hearing. I remember picking up the newspaper and seeing a picture of them, the union officials and the internal affairs personnel all huddled in the train station office where the brutality occurred. I was never notified. When I asked about it, I was told by the department advocate that my testimony was not necessary.

Just prior to that, the acting Police Chief and our Union President were both featured in a Connecticut Post article. Neither condemned the treatment I was receiving from my fellow Officers. One had the nerve to say that it would be a while before anyone trusted me again. The other said that Daniels made an unpopular decision. I believe them not condemning the retaliation acts toward me, lead to more spit on my car and boosted the backs being turned on me. One Officer even tried to run me over with a police car, but I jumped out of the way. I said nothing to those in charge. Instead, I continued working and waiting for the school year to begin so that I could teach the D.A.R.E. program.

Because of all the racial problems and Bridgeport Guardian lawsuits, the Special Master that oversaw the department decided to review the incidences that I was complaining about. A special inquiry would have to be held, but it nixed, because the Feds decided to indict the brutality Officer on civil rights charges. I was now aware that I was still facing departmental charges myself for not reporting the incident in a timely manner. So much was happening and it was a difficult period, to say the least.

I had another interview with the FBI and the Justice department shortly after a grand jury was convened in Hartford about the civil rights charges. Me and the other named officers were called to testify. The night before court, I was told that one of the other officers that were on scene was going to step up and do the right thing. Of course, it was only after he had some serious thought about the possibility of him being looked into by the same agencies. He was supposed to pretty much corroborate the testimony that I was going to give in open court. Around this time, I was served with divorce papers. I felt sorry for Yvette living with me at that time. It could not have been easy. I was

DAVID DANIELS, III

very emotional and cried a lot. I could get very angry with very little stimulus. No matter which way I turned, I just couldn't get away from this. But Yvette, she hung in there with me for as long as she could. I wasn't getting much support from my fellow black Officers. I just wanted this to be over, so that I could go back to my normal life. I didn't know it at the time, but my life was never to be the same again.

The morning of the Grand Jury hearing in Hartford, I was awaked by two loud explosions outside my home. I knew they were meant for me, because when I looked out of my bedroom window, my car alarm was the only one blaring with the lights flashing. I jumped up, showered, shaved and put on a Blue suit to head to Hartford. I was paranoid and kept thinking about someone trying to kill me. I got to Hartford, parked the car and looked all around then ran into the courthouse as fast as I could. Once inside, I was ushered into the courtroom, gave my testimony, answered all of the lawyer's questions and then returned home to my apartment in West Haven.

The next day's papers exclaimed that the brutality Officer was implicated and now a trial would be forthcoming. Every time a new story was printed in the paper, without fail, things would get worse for me. Soon, no one within the department would be talking to me, black or white. I felt like a man without a country. Just two days later, I am assigned to a two-man overtime walking patrol job at The Trumbull Gardens Housing Project. I am the first to arrive for the second shift, so I go inside the building where the police have an office setup. Once I get in the office, I see a few other Officers are still hanging around from the first shift.

About two hours late, a veteran Officer from my old platoon shows up to work the shift with me. As he walks in, he looks at every other person in the room and speaks.

"What's up? What's going on?"

He says to this officer and to that officer. Then to them all, he says.

"How we looking tonight?"

BLACK & BLUE IN BRIDGEPORT

I am beside myself. He greeted everyone present, except me. I do not get it, but I do not say anything in front of the group.

A few moments later, we hear gunfire outside. We all run outside from the office and spread out all around the building. We are all looking around in different directions, this way and that way, but neither of us seeing anyone. Not a single person. No one is shooting or even holding a gun. Once we give each other the 'all clear' we all begin to walk back toward the building. My old platoon buddy is walking near me and we are away from everyone else. I look to him and make my statement.

"Wow, you're not speaking to me either?"

I did not give him a chance to respond, I just continued.

"I can accept why some people don't speak, but they don't know me, but you do! We are from the same platoon, we rode together. I thought we were friends?"

Holding a blank expression, he stops walking so I stop also. He looks up and into my face and speaks with a low tone.

"I don't know you! We are not friends and I could never respect you. You fucked with that man's livelihood."

Then, he looks me up and down. With my and face full of disgust from what I just heard, I quickly reply.

"If you can respect someone that beats on people in handcuffs, then you can take your respect and shove it up your ass!"

I stand there waiting for his reply. He chomps down on his cigar, says nothing and storms off into the building. For the next six hours remaining on the shift, we work in total silence, while trying not to even look at each other.

By this is time, working with an Officer or alone was made difficult for me. On another shift at the same housing project, I was by myself and I could have used some backup. There was a car accident in which a child crossing the street had been struck by a car. A crowd began to form quickly and someone in the crowd wanted to beat up the driver.

DAVID DANIELS, III

Although I warned them not to that, the crowd continued moving forward, but I was able to call for additional cars and an ambulance just in time.

One of the few times I was able to get through on the radio, I thanked the other Officer for responding. This one female Officer was standing near some kids that knew me from teaching DARE in their school. They overheard her say something to other cops mulling around.

"Fuck Daniels, he thinks we came to back him up."

When they described her to me, I knew immediately who they were talking about. I got so upset that I reported her to my superiors, but nothing was done. Things would continue just like this, time after time, call after call. There were countless incidents, but most of them I would never mention.

I was soon called before the Board of Police Commissioners about the charge brought against me concerning the train station incident. I was being charged with not reporting the incident of brutality in a timely manner. As I learned, I should have reported it on that day, before I completed my shift. Now I had to appear before the board to answer the charge. These types of meetings are held in the Police Chief's office and open to the public. The newspaper had published an article explaining what was going on the day before. I came in and sat down at the front table, then people started coming in and took up every seat. Soon the room was at capacity with people occupying every bit of space in the room. People I had never seen before, black and white. My mother, ex-wife and Guardian members were there. Even people that I worked with at the telephone company showed up. Most of them either held miniature American flags in their hands or wore red, white and blue ribbons on their clothing. All the local media was there as well.

Confronted with all that humanity in the room, the Board offered me a deal. If I plead no contest to the charge of not reporting the train station in a timely manner, I would receive no discipline. I asked them during a hushed moment that if I took the deal would I be able to address the crowd. They agreed, so I took the deal.

I quietly stood and told the people gathered in that office all about what I had been through. That I had been feeling alone since this whole ordeal started, but that changed when I saw all of them show up this evening. I told them that I could not convey in words how they had lifted my spirits and I freely admitted not reporting the incident in a timely matter. I did most of that talking with tears streaming down my face. The Board President then stated to the crowd that I would not be disciplined and then they all begin to cheer.

Although the cheers from the crowd felt warm at that moment, it had been a long journey for me to get there. Only after I was forced to admit to not telling anyone in a timely matter, could I escape discipline. Unlike the brutality Officer, who would retire and have all charges dropped. Or the other two Officers implicated that were found innocent of all charges. By the way, neither of them ever reported the incident at all, but escaped the charge that I was forced to admit to in my hearing.

In time, Toni and I were divorced. I was still depressed and emotionally drained most of time even though things on the street had changed. People on the street were smiling at me, reaching out to me shaking my hand, and patting me on the back. They were breaking their necks to say something positive to me. I went to see the Guardians Lawyer at the offices of Koskoff, Koskoff and Beider and while on the elevator, a smartly dressed white man asked me if I was Officer Daniels. I apprehensively said yes, and then him and other people in the elevator started to applaud me and patted me on the back. I just stood there not knowing what to do or say. The doors opened and off I went into the lawyer's office.

It now seemed almost common for me to turn on a radio and hear my name or pick up a newspaper and see my likeness. Politicians and

DAVID DANIELS, III

Clergy were calling to offer support, as were gangsters to thank me for being a real brother. They all wanted to let me know that they had my back. Bridgeport's NAACP Chairman called the press and went on record expressing his outrage about how I had been treated by the police department. The Board of Police Commissioners' Chairman Marcia Goodman let her feelings be known as well. That year a black organization named its community service award after me. If I attended a Bridgeport church, I was singled out or asked to say a few words. If I attended any public function, I would hear my name over the PA as being in attendance. I didn't realize it then, but my life had changed and would never be the same.

During that next summer, I was able to do Officer Friendly visits to daycare centers and camps. I stood and spoke at Crime Patrol Groups and even church gatherings. Everywhere I went people wanted me to talk about the train station incident. I worked at John Bagley's Basketball Camp, I was an M.C. at the Save Our Babies summer festival at Seaside Park and I played in a few celebrity basketball games. But mostly, I tried to spend a lot of my free time at home away from people.

While at home, I started receiving harassing phone calls every day. The FBI was again supposed to monitoring the situation, but they didn't even notice when I changed my phone number three times to relieve the situation. I guess I never learned to live being paranoid, because it was hard. I moved several times and never got comfortable. To this day, I still get nervous when to many people know my whereabouts.

When September rolled around and school started, I picked out the schools where I would be teaching D.A.R.E. I choose four schools; Park City Magnet, Roosevelt, Blessed Sacrament and Longfellow. I choose each of them because they were in or near a housing project in our city. Blessed Sacrament wasn't near a housing project, but in was in the hood. I set up my schedule so I could be at Longfellow School first. It was right across the street from P.T. Barnum Housing Projects where I had grown up. I went to school there from kindergarten to the third grade. I was extremely nervous when I entered the classroom. But as I quickly learned the children's names, I came to realize that I knew people in their families and had grown up with some of their parents. All the teachers that I had were generally helpful to me starting out. Over the course of eight years, I would teach thousands of Bridgeport Kids the program before I was done. Besides having my own children and becoming a police officer, teaching that program was one of the things I will forever be most proud of.

During my time in the Community Services Division, I won awards to numerous to mention. My work allowed me to travel the country extensively. This included returning to some cities more than once on both coasts and even teaching down south. I guess it may be true, that every cloud has a silver lining, because being in that department made me happy. So, in this position is where I remained, until I took and passed the Sergeants' exam.

DAVID DANIELS, III

BLACK & BLUE IN BRIDGEPORT

DAVID DANIELS, III

Chapter VIII
The Seventies
Growing Up

It was an exciting time to be alive. I was coming of age, the world was changing and history was being made. I started high school at Bassick High in 1970. I was fourteen years old. Standing just four feet and eleven inches, I started my freshman year very immature and full of energy. But that summer before, I had discovered basketball.

It was a summer day, my mother sent me out into the complex to find my brother Reggie to bring him home. Although P.T. Barnum was a low housing complex, there were recreational areas for us to play. There was the park at the top of the drive that had plenty of grass and a jungle gym with slides. Then there were the basketball courts down at the bottom of the drive, across the street near Longfellow Elementary School. That's where I found Reggie, at the basketball courts.

Reggie was on the court in the middle of playing a game with his friends. I walked up to the four foot fence that enclosed the courts and just watched them all play. After a while, this one kid just up and quit. Not wanting to stop the game, they looked around for another player and saw me, so they asked me to take his place. I accepted, even though I didn't know how to play.

Whenever they threw me the ball, I would try to mimic things I had seen Oscar Robertson doing on television during NBA games.

I was having the time of my life. All the while, thinking I was doing pretty good, but I was wrong. In reality, I was double dribbling, carrying the ball and throwing up some pretty wild shots. Even though I was having a great time, I was also embarrassing Reggie, who was a seasoned player by now.

Then without any notice, the game suddenly came to an abrupt stop. I looked around to see why everyone just stopped and now standing at the fence where I had been admiring the guys play, was my mother. Unlike me, she had that mad mother look on her face, a belt in her hand and a trail of kids following behind her that wanted to see who was going to get beaten. All of sudden, I remembered what I was told to do. Looking directly at me, my mother yelled from the fence.

"Didn't I tell you to go get your brother and come home?"

At that point I knew we were in trouble. I tried to defect my mother's attention to Reggie, so I pointed at him. As I turned to look at him, I saw that he was pointing at me. Realizing what was coming next and how we didn't want it to happen in front of our friends, we both tried to run off toward our building. She didn't run after us. Instead, my mother called us back to her. Cautiously we came back, but stood just out of belt reach.

"Don't you ever run away from me!"

My mother then proceeded to wear us both out with that belt. Still wanting to run, we dared not to until we got closer to our building. After getting off punishment for that incident, almost every day I could be found at the basketball courts, with permission, of course.

On one of those cool summer days, I rode my five-speed bike to the courts to play some ball. There were always other kids there playing and I would just join in. After we finished a game, I noticed that this girl named Nydia had been sitting on one of the concrete benches watching us play.

When I jumped on my bike to go home, she called out to me.

"Can you give me a ride?"

I didn't really know what to say, but I didn't mind giving her a ride, so I said the first thing that came to mind.

"Okay."

She walked over and jumped on my bike and we rode off toward my building. When we arrived, she got off and thanked me for the ride. We stood there and looking at each other for a moment. She didn't live in my building and it didn't look like she was ready to walk off. I didn't know what else to say, but I wanted to say something.

"I'm going to take my bike upstairs and I'll be right back, okay?"

I thought I could walk her to her building after I put my bike up. But she didn't just agree. Instead, she asked another question.

"Can I just come up with you?"

Thinking nothing of it again, I just replied without a care.

"Okay."

When we got to the third floor and I turned the knob on the door, it was locked. This only meant one thing, no one was home. I unlocked the door with my key and we both strolled inside. She sat down on the couch and I made my way to the kitchen, like normal. On the refrigerator was a note from my mother telling me that she had taken my brothers and sisters and went downtown.

Since we didn't have a car, they had to take the city buses. First, the Barnum Avenue bus then transfer to the State Street bus, just to get there. Then, the time to do all the walking around and shopping, plus the two bus rides to get back meant, they would be gone for hours.

To this day I don't remember whose idea it was, but somehow we ended up on my bed hugging and then kissing. Next thing I know, all our clothes are off and we are under the covers. I really had no idea what I was doing. I guess it was just moving on instinct. Fumbled at my first attempt to penetrate, but she guided me on the second attempt.

While thrusting myself inside her, I was experiencing something so pleasurable that I didn't even know how it was possible. When I climaxed, I somehow knew that things would be different for me now.

BLACK & BLUE IN BRIDGEPORT

A milestone to manhood, that was unplanned and a total surprise. Lying there, we smiled at each other. It was a game changer, a watershed moment and all that.

Staring up at the ceiling, I played it over in my mind like a million times. She then hopped out of bed and sprinted to the bathroom. Like a teenage boy would, I still laying there and smelling my fingers with a big smile on my face. Finally, I got dressed and walked her home.

On my way back, I was on cloud nine. Although I couldn't believe what had happened, I was happy that it did. Then reality struck! I started thinking about all the what ifs? What if, I got her pregnant? What if she gave me a venereal disease? I didn't know the answer to either question, so I quickly dismissed both notions and went back to the good thoughts of having my first sexual experience.

No one was home, so I changed my mind about there and ran all the way back down to the basketball courts. I told my friends that I had just got some. Like boys do, they challenged me on it. So, I let them smell my fingers. They tried to get me to tell them who I was with. I didn't tell them about Nydia or that it was my first time. They were happy for me and we all walked up to the Beverly Pizza House and celebrated with a pizza.

Nydia and I had been friends since kindergarten. Even to this day, I don't know if she knew back then that she was my first. I'll never forget her from that day or how wonderful it was. While we continued to see each other around, we never talked about it or had sex with each other again. I thought about saying something to her about it over the years, because I really wanted to, but I never did.

PLAYING BASKETBALL was becoming a pure joy for me. After a while I got better. Slowly developing adequate skills to compete with kids that were my age and size, but I wanted to be better. So I moved on to playing with older, bigger and quicker guys. At first it was tough, they were so much better than me. They would push me all over the court and take the ball from me. Post me up and down low and straight burning me with jumpers out on the wings. I hadn't figured out how to defend against these guys yet, but I didn't quit. Finally, I reached a level where I could compete and hold my own with anyone that stepped on the court with me.

Around this time, I started to grow and on the court I had a quick first step to the basket. That's when I discovered jumping up to the rim and forcing the ball down through the basket. In the 1960's this was called dunking and it was outlawed at the collegiate level. Back then, basketball was all about strategy and a player's floor game. Point guards controlled the game. People like Oscar Robertson, Bob Cousy and Dave Bing were ground game stars.

A player performing a perfect dunk shot during a game was almost unstoppable and that made people fearful. This fear was centered on players like Lew Alcindor and Wilt Chamberlain and how they could use it to dominate the game. When it was finally allowed, it took the game to the air. This brought us new stars like 'Jumping' Johnny Green, Connie Hawkins and eventually Dr. J. Dunking is what drove basketball's revolution and evolution down the road to becoming a global sport icon. Stars like George Gervin, David Thompson and Julius Dr. J. Erving were brought in our homes when the NBA and ABA leagues merged. The other sport attraction back then was in boxing with Muhammad Ali. I enjoyed boxing, but not as much as watching my favorite basketball player, Dr. J. Erving.

When I wasn't playing basketball, I use to get excited about watching movies, right at home. This was a sweeping time for entertainment and black actor driven movies. These films were filled with constant action scenes and music that kept my attention. I was happy to see black people in leading roles and cheering as the anti-establishment plots played out in the favor of black people overcoming the powers that be.

BLACK & BLUE IN BRIDGEPORT

It was in 1971 that Melvin Van Peebles premiered the movie Sweetback's Baadassss Song. This movie helped usher in a slew of other blaxploitation films. These types of movies featured super Negro characters prevailing over police brutality, racism and the ghetto itself. The movies were everywhere and I saw many of them. Cotton Comes To Harlem, Shaft, Shaft in Africa, Trouble Man, Nigga Charlie, Across 110th Street, Black Caesar and many, many more. Equally, there were other great movies like Sounder and Claudine that were more serious and focused on the real struggles of black people in this country.

Right out of Bridgeport, came our very own Christopher St. John, who played the character Ben in the first Shaft Movie. His son Krisstoff St. John also grew up to be a premier soap opera actor as well. Christopher's brother, Charles Smith, was a Bridgeport Police officer and his son Charles D. Smith played professional basketball for The LA Clippers, San Antonio Spurs and New York Knicks.

Lighting up the mood came with the Karate films that kicked off in the country. Generations of ghetto children could be seen kicking and karate chopping each other leaving theatres all over the hood. Such films made television actor Bruce Lee into a superstar.

Nevertheless, the cries of more learned blacks began to surface. Outraged and disappointed, they belittled the blaxploitation films because of their stereotypical impact. Just watching them for pure entertainment, I did not understand their upset completely, so I would hear none of that. As a matter of fact, no one would ever argue that it wasn't some of the best music ever recorded, for the time. As for my time, I would eventually come to understand and agree that these films did more damage for black people overall, than good. Even with all the complaints, it must be noted that the worst of these films still had some great music attached to them. Like Curtis Mayfield's Super Fly, Isaac Hayes' theme song from Shaft and Marvin Gaye's Trouble Man soundtrack, to name a few.

DAVID DANIELS, III

Music was changing as well. Around 1975, rap music was gaining popularity. My formal introduction to the genre came in 1979 when I first heard the group called The Sugar Hill Gang. Their song, Rapper's Delight was on a DJ tape released on a twelve inch single. It was about ten minutes long and featured the music of Chic's Good Times in the background. The group had three guys; Big Bank Hank, Wonder Mike and Master G talking over the music, saying rhymes. At first, I thought it was a novelty record, but time proved how wrong I was.

Rapper's Delight is the song that ushered in the birth of hip-hop music. In present day, its contribution is still acknowledged in the industry. Through its usage in sampling, mixing and scratching in all genres of new songs including jazz and rock, it continues to flourish. Unlike hip-hop, disco came thru during the era as well, but it had a short life in comparison. Having the pleasure later in life, I would meet and befriend one of hip-hop's pioneers, DJ Tony Tone aka Tony Crush. He is the creator of The Cold Crush Brothers.

My freshman year was at Norfolk State University and it was a trying one. Having now grown to be six feet and one inch tall, it was my first time being away from home and no learning not to depend on my mother. The change was big and a personal growth period for me.

I had to make adult decisions for myself, feed myself, and provide overall care for myself. I would be meeting people from all over the United States and foreign countries as well. I met southern, western and eastern black people with their respective accents, mannerisms, beliefs and styles. I was like a sponge soaking it all in.

Norfolk State was nestled right in the heart of the city of Norfolk, Virginia. It was open and accessible to the surrounding community. I really grew up there mentally and physically. I majored in Communications. My required courses like English, Math, Arts and Sciences, I did okay. In my electives; Introduction to Media, Radio and Television Production and Public Speaking, I excelled.

BLACK & BLUE IN BRIDGEPORT

I remember my first day in television production class when the professor stood in front of us all and said this:

"Some of you will not be here in four years. Some of you won't be here in two years. Some of you will never use the skills you acquire here, and more importantly, some of you will never work in media."

Listening to those words made me want to excel in all my media classes. On one project in television production, I was chosen to be the director of a project and I did my best. From there, I was then chosen to direct a short film for the consumption of incoming high school students. This was an annual event and I jumped in with both feet. Picking classmates to be on my team, I chose the best camera operator, edit mixer and audio technician in the class. The film we produced gave the students a birds-eye view of the television production department and what we did there. As a result, our grade was an A. Personally I was very proud of myself and how the process helped unmask my leadership skills. The professor was right. Becoming a police officer was as far away from working in media as I could get, but he was also wrong. The skills I learned in those classes would stay with me and I would choose to use them as often as I could.

Being there at Norfolk State was my first taste of seeing black people in charge of institutions. The school's administration was predominantly black as were the teachers and support staff. This made my heart swell with pride. We even ate grits for breakfast, cooked by black kitchen workers and collard greens for dinner, served by those same loving hands.

As for partying, we didn't have to go far. Right on campus there were campus parties everywhere. We jammed to the sounds of The Jimmy Castor Bunch, Parliament Funkadelic, Earth, Wind & Fire and Bootsy's Rubber Band. My school was the 'Kings of the CIAA.' In collegiate sports, we were number one in football, basketball, baseball and even track. Boasting with players like Steve Riddick in Olympic Track and Field, Ron Brown in the National Football League and Bob

DAVID DANIELS, III

Dandridge in the National Basketball Association. Even in music, The Wooten Brothers and The Band Mass Production were groups formed in the Norfolk area. Not to forget, Norfolk State also had some of the most beautiful women that I had ever seen.

My first year at Norfolk State, I lived in the dormitories on campus with a roommate. He was a native New Yorker named Gerald Henry Mason. Gerald was from Brooklyn and he once played basketball with legendary NBA great Nate 'Tiny' Archibald. He was a sophomore and also a communications major. He was my guide and helped me get acclimated to our department.

Gerald also introduced me to music from the artist Larry Graham. Graham is the former bass guitar player for the group Sly and The Family Stone. He explained how Graham had been a DJ at one point in his life and how he left the group to form his own. The group he formed was named Graham Central Station.

So, when Grand Central Station released the song titled 'The Jam', I was ready. It was the party record of that year. It conjures up memories of Sly and the Family Stone's song 'Dance To The Music' to me. A song so collectively funky, that is driven by isolated contributions highlighted and interwoven from each individual group member to create one phenomenally funky track. Graham would eventually become a solo act laboring to give us such classics as 'One In A Million' and 'When We Get Married.' Being at Norfolk State was exposing me to all kinds of new things. It was the best of times, but then came the worst of times.

My life at Norfolk State was great and I really lucked out that year having Gerald as a roommate. Not only was he a good guy, he owned a car and had it with him on campus. One upcoming weekend, he was planning on going home to New York for a few days. Knowing that I was from Connecticut, he offered me a ride to New York, if I wanted to go home that weekend and I accepted. Catching a Greyhound bus from there, I made it to Bridgeport. While home for a few days, I saw family,

BLACK & BLUE IN BRIDGEPORT

spent time with my girlfriend, played basketball with my friends and partied a little bit. Returning to New York on Sunday, Gerald picked me up at the bus station and we hit Interstate 95 South, heading back to Virginia. After a pretty much uneventful eight hour drive, we made it to the city of Norfolk, but we got off at the wrong exit. Driving around in circles for a while, I guess we were looking suspicious, so we were stopped by a patrol car.

By now, it was around 10 p.m., on a cold and dark Sunday night. We were told to exit the vehicle with our hands over our heads and we did as we were told. As I was getting out, I remember how bright and intense all the flashing lights were. Although we couldn't tell how many patrol cars were behind us, as soon as they could, the officers began manhandling us. Grabbing on us and forcing us to the ground, as if we were fighting or resisting their demands. There had to be at least five or even six officers on the scene.

We tried telling them that we were students at Norfolk State. They responded by telling us to shut up, so we did. Pressed up against the car, I start looking around. I saw officers holding shotguns. I felt my heart beating through my chest and heavy sweat dripping down my face, like I had just walked off a basketball court.

Cops were going through our pockets and finding nothing. We both were placed in handcuffs and make to sit on the curb. Gerald and I both didn't say another word to the officers. They took our school identifications and got on the radio to check us out. One officer finally started to tell us that there had been a robbery in the area. Gerald and I just looked at each other and without words, understood what was really going on. The officer continued by saying that they had seen us driving around the area in a car with New York plates and that is why we were stopped.

After what seemed like hours, one officer tells us to stand up and he un-cuffed us as he says we were free to leave. I could feel the adrenaline coursing thru my veins and could barely walk back to the car, because my legs felt like jelly. Once back inside the car, the patrol cars escorted us back to the highway. I didn't know about Gerald, but this was my first run in with the local authorities. Gerald and I didn't speak another word as we continued the drive back to campus. The shock of what had just happened to us was overwhelming. Although we did not want to believe it, we had to accept it and we were embarrassed. The only good thing to come out the run-in was neither of us ever got lost again, within the city of Norfolk, Virginia.

Completing my sophomore year, I was eager to begin my adult life and take my place in this world, so I made the hard decision not to return to school the following year. Although I still had not shared my desires about becoming a police officer with anyone at home, I did tell a female about them, before I left. Her reaction was typical, as I would soon come to accept. It seems that no one ever congratulates you for having such thoughts. For most people, the thought of choosing a profession where your chances of getting killed are increased, is considered simply crazy.

Those two years at Norfolk State were big ones in my life, but I was ready to move on. Once I moved back to Bridgeport, I would never see Gerald Henry Mason again. There would come times when I wondered what happened to him and how his life turned out, but I never looked him up. Just as before I left for college, being back in Bridgeport made it easy to return to suppressing my desires and ideas of becoming a police officer.

Over that first summer at home, I worked a seasonal job as an Assistant Director in the A.B.C.D. Summer Camp program. Held at Longfellow School, which was across the street from P.T., I held off telling my mother that I wasn't returning to school until the last possible minute and that minute came in August. She was hurt and disappointed, but she didn't let me know how much.

My mother was always in my corner. She has been my biggest cheerleader and always proud of what I was able to accomplish. Now I

BLACK & BLUE IN BRIDGEPORT

was telling her I wasn't going back to school and that didn't make her happy, but she always trusted my judgment. When I told her I wanted to get a job instead, she understood, because she always allowed me to make my own decisions.

In September, I started putting in job applications everywhere all over town. My first interview came up at Sears and Roebuck in The Lafayette Plaza in downtown Bridgeport. I was excited. Choosing my best button down shirt, tie and Stacey Adams shoes with my educated Negro attitude, I promptly secured a part time job in the Marketing Department. Unfortunately, I had made a big mistake and had to quit after that first day. I was so disappointed, I never returned to collect my wages. While I thought I was going to be working in the Marketing Department, I was assigned to the Marking Department and was responsible for putting prices on the merchandise.

I then interviewed and was offered a position as a bank teller at The City Trust Bank, right downtown. I would have accepted that position, because it was so high profile. With my love of clothes and getting dressed up for work, being a bank teller would have allowed for me to look good all day. But then I realized, the meager wages would not support all the dry cleaning I would accrue, so I declined.

My girlfriend, at that time, began to pressure me about getting a job. She was ready to unveil our wedding plans to her family and it would not sit well with them that I was unemployed. The same held true for me back when I told my mother I wasn't going back to school. I chose not reveal our plans to her for the same reason. With this in mind and the pressure, I took the very next job offer I got.

The Southern New England Telephone Company, affectionately called SNET had positions open for telephone operators. Over the next eleven years, I was an SNET employee. I held various positions like; an operator, general office clerk, cable splicer's helper and a business representative. Over all, my stint at SNET was frustrating.

DAVID DANIELS, III

I loved working with some of my co-workers, but I didn't like the company as much.

For my first three years, I was an operator and this was the company's intention. Being male, in this position, made it a non-traditional placement. The world again, was changing and callers would now hear male voices on the phone when they needed operators and also see women installing telephones. While there, I had a front seat watching the government break up the Southern New England Bell system of the monopoly that they had in the telephone communications industry. It was called divestiture and the breakup of the 'Ma Bell'. I would be right there, during all of the changes going on all around us.

As a male operator, I would be called a pioneer. I would endure customer verbal assaults on my manhood on one hand, while fending off customer propositions on the other. The company was strict and the employees had to deal with it every day. We needed permission to go to the restrooms or just to leave the areas where we worked. When leaving, we had to turn on this light which let the other employees know that no one could leave at that time. Upon returning, we had to turn the light off, so anyone that needed to leave could do so. We couldn't talk to the operator sitting next to us, this was a punishable offense. If your break started at 1 p.m., we could not leave our work stations until 12:59 p.m. Additionally, if your break ended at 1:15 p.m., you needed to be seated at 1:14 p.m., with no exceptions.

The company didn't tolerate tardiness at all, which made it very hard for many employees. I was able to endure this environment by working split-shifts or taking what was called AX time. This time occurred when you were working your shift and there was a surplus of workers compared to the work load. One could request AX time and if approved, then leave without completing their shift, without pay.

On the bright side, there were perks from working there. Only because of the job security, its benefits and the retirement package, I endured my time there. Their benefits made it possible for me to plan a real future. I shored up my wardrobe, brought three brand new cars, provided for my family and this allowed me to take my place in this world. Before my last day, it had been just three days shy of eleven years there. My time at SNET was only coming to an end because it was time for me to finally become a police officer.

As I knew the police department would be contacting my job to inquire about me, I finally told my supervisor that I would be leaving to become a Bridgeport police officer. My supervisor Colleen looked me in the face and simply asked me.

"Why would you leave the security of SNET to take such a dangerous job in Bridgeport?"

I understood her reaction, because it was in line with the limited few I had already mentioned it to. Usually, I would just hear their response and not reply, but this time was different. I explained to her that becoming a police officer had always been my dream and that I was just following my heart. As for staying at the telephone company, I didn't see my future prospects there being as great because of the changes deregulation had caused. She listened as I expressed my belief in how I would have the opportunity to positively impact lives, especially the lives of children, if I took this chance. That day, I shared my excitement about what I was about to do with Colleen and I was happy about it. Even if she didn't understand, what was really clear is that nothing was possible until, when and because, I left SNET.

Chapter IX
Officer Lawbreaker
Meat or Grass Eater

Last week I was watching the HBO Mini Series The Deuce. The drama series centers on the porno industry during the 1970s and 1980s. Set in the old Times Square area of New York City, it weaves its story line through the Mafia, peep shows, pornographic films, pimps, prostitutes, massage parlors and corrupt corporations. In the first two episodes, they portray the officers as being on the take and being a big part of the sleazy culture of that time period. There is a scene in the seventh episode, when a new Captain that is assigned to the precinct, makes contact with a black Officer that's assigned to patrol. He asks the Officer to show him the area around 42nd Street. While they are touring the area, he asks him; are you a Meat Eater or a Grass Eater?

The black Officer looks at him puzzled and asks what does that mean? The Captain explains that he wants to clean up the precinct and that he needs his help. The black Officer asks him why me? The Captain replies by telling him that someone higher up told him that if you really want to find out what is going on in a department you should talk to a black officer. The Officer asked him why a black officer? The Captain exclaimed that more than likely, a black officer would know what was going on and have the moral compass to not be a part of it. He went on to state, that he could use that officers desire to make rank to garner support for his endeavors to clean things up. The Captain goes on to leave the black Officer with a serious declaration: There is two kinds of officers on the force, Meat Eaters and Grass Eaters.

Grass Eaters - police officers that involve themselves in minor corruption like; taking free meals, taking free coffee, taking discounts on things that have a greater value, utilizing services and not paying the normal costs or fees for anything.

Meat Eaters - police officers that engage in major corruption like; shaking down businesses, robbing drug dealers, extorting monies from any people and doing other shady things that negatively affect the masses of people they are sworn to protect.

I had not heard that term since the time I read a book on police management, back while I studied to take my first promotional exam for the rank of Sergeant. In my experience, it seemed hard for most officers to avoid falling into being one of the types, for one reason or another. The logic being; that in many police departments, once an officer becomes a grass eater, the likelihood of graduating to becoming a meat eater, seemed less threatening.

It reminded me of an instance. Back when a new McDonald's restaurant was built out on the city's west end. It was rumored that employees would give officers free food so there could always be a police car in there parking lot. After about two months of their grand opening, the rumor made it up the chain of command. The Police Chief responded by dispatching a black Sergeant to the location just to sit there and watch the establishment. During the few hours, he sat and watched as several police cars frequent the restaurant. After a few days of watching this business' activity, he had the answer to the rumor. He reported back to the Chief that the rumors were in fact true and that the business was giving officers free food.

Upon getting this report, the Chief himself, ventured to the restaurant and demanded to the owner to stop feeding the officers for free. The owner replied to the Chief's demand by telling him that it was his business and he would conduct it as he saw fit. That in fact, he would continue serving the officers free food. The Chief returned to Police Headquarters and issued a memorandum forbidding officers to even go to the restaurant in uniform or while on duty. Officers that wanted to continue to take advantage were in luck. The restaurant employees remembered most of the cops by face or if you showed the badge, they continued passing out free food.

This was a common practice amongst the local businesses, once they became aware that you were an officer. Most would give the officer the food for free or charged very little for it. I never paid more than a dime for all the small coffees I enjoyed during my career. I never paid to get into any local bar or club, no matter what the cover was. I remember having a business meeting with a few civilians at a local restaurant. There were four or five of us and we ate very well. When the bill came and it was time to pay, the total bill was just fifteen dollars. I took the receipt and just paid it. All the while, the people in attendance were in awe, because all that they ate did not reflect in what we were actually charged.

In general terms, the grass eaters stayed away from the meat eaters. For most officers understood that meat eaters hardly ever made it to their retirement and pension. Unfortunately, their greed often got them discovered, forced out, fired or worse.

I knew officers that would take all of the cassette tapes or CDs that they discovered in recovered stolen cars. If a place got burglarized, like a liquor store or business with valuable commodities in it, sometimes the officers would cart off more than the burglars once they arrived. As time wore on, business owners started incorporating more sophisticated alarms systems with sound equipment and cameras, which diminished this practice. In one instance here in Bridgeport, a business security system intercepted an incident. One of our officers let a burglar go after catching on him the premises and in the act. Believe it or not, that officer did not even get fired after that violation. The whole conversation was captured by listening devices activated during the break in.

During my time on the job, I know of an officer that I met at D.A.R.E. school that was from another town. While on duty, he went on a midnight burglary call to a business that sold frozen seafood to restaurants. When the officer arrived, the burglar had taken whatever it was that he could carry and already ran off. The officer then backs his patrol car up to the building and loaded the police car with all that he could gather. To his determent, he never realized that all of his actions were being recorded by video and sound. Within a year after, he was fired. Unfortunately, with non-disclosure agreements being what they are, he was able to join another force and is still working as a police officer, somewhere else.

Chapter X
White Before Blue
Internal Infestation

The Bridgeport Police Department is known by its long history of being one of the most racist institutions in the city. Prior to me joining the force, I knew of that history way back when I was in high school. I use to absorb all those newspaper articles that were written back in the early 70's. They spoke about The Bridgeport Guardians, along with the Law firm of Koskoff, Koskoff and Beider and how they had the department in court trying to change the department for the better. My experiences were not solely about the racism. Although I mention it, in the situations where it showed itself, I chose not to dwell on it or make it the majority of my experiences. For those white officers that were clearly making sure that white officers held the upper hand in any and all situations, you know who you are. I honestly believe, not all my white counterparts were trying to find ways to treat black officers differently every day. They themselves were simply caught up in a system that favored them and/or gave them full-time privilege and advantage over everyone else. Since they never felt any negative impact, they could not relate to us or what our problems were. For those that really want to know, here is one glaring experience of mine. I only offer you this instance for you to consider. Use it as an example of what we, black officers, faced everyday going to work there.

BLACK & BLUE IN BRIDGEPORT

For months it had been announced that our first black President, Barack Obama, would be coming to Bridgeport during a campaign stop to address a crowd to be assembled at our Webster Bank Arena. Our Chief dispatched a white Lieutenant and Sergeant to work with the Secret Service and the government to fashion a detailed operation to cover this visit. A part of the plan was to interface with the government agencies in charge of the President's security to plan how we would cover the President's arrival at our City Airport in the neighboring town in Stratford. Then include logistical and geographical planning to cover the motorcade ride to the arena, security at the venue and an exit plan to egress from the building back to the motorcade then return to the airport.

A couple of weeks before commencement of this event, the Chief called a series of meetings to further the planning process along. In a final meeting, just a day before the visit, the whole upper command staff met alone. After this meeting, everyone else would be told what our individual assignments were and where we would be placed in the detail. We were to learn what sector we would cover, what subordinates would be under our command and what their function was to be. I was told that the only black Captain in the department, the other two black Lieutenants and I would be the only officers stationed at the front of the building. Right away my 'Spidey' sense started to tingle. Effectively, these assignments left us to only supervise one another and this made no sense, so I made a mental note it, but said nothing. Additionally, we were told no pictures would be allowed and that we could not enter the building at any point during this visit. In the event that we needed relief, we were to travel back to police headquarters and then return to post outside of the building.

When event day arrived, a few hours before the President was to land, we gathered in the City Hall's parking lot for any last minute instructions for the patrolman assigned to the motorcade and for inspection, before we all left for our detail. When the white Lieutenant and Sergeant arrived to address the detail, I noticed that they both had fresh haircuts and were wearing formal police attire. At no time during any of our meetings had it be discussed or had we been instructed to wear our formal attire. I looked around and saw other white personnel of varying rank also in formal dress. Then it dawned on me. They were all positioned so they could at least see or be seen by the President.

Noticing this, I started to get angry. While we were on sight, I talked to the other officers at my post and impressed upon them the situation that we had been put in. The planners of the event expected a crowd of ten-thousand or more to attend. The contingency plan was to put the spillover crowd in the neighboring building that was the city's Bluefish Baseball Stadium. There were jumbo-trons set up so the people ushered into that space could see the full address as it transpired. The plan included that the President would pop into the stadium for a minute, prior to taking the main stage at the Webster Bank Arena. I told the black Captain and the other two Lieutenants that if the President popped into the stadium for a minute, I would like to see him there and they agreed to go over as well.

Because the crowd just barely made the ten-thousand people, there was not going to be a Presidential pop in. In the meantime, the Captain needed to go to the bathroom, so he jumped in his car and drove the distance to police headquarters. Once the Captain returned, one of the Lieutenants left only to return a little while later in his formal police attire. I then told the others that after the President was inside the venue, under the pretext of having to go to the bathroom, I was going inside. I also stated that I was not going to let them stop me from at least seeing our first black president in person, with my own eyes. They reminded me that we were told by the white Lieutenant not to enter the building and that the Secret Service would not allow us to enter. I told them that the Secret Service's uniformed police officers would respect our rank, even if our own department did not. So we should not have any problems going into the building. I then further explained that in any case, we could not be brought up on charges. Because the person that told us that we could not go inside was of equal rank and in the case of the Captain, he clearly out ranked that Lieutenant.

In the front of the building was a rather large crowd. They were pretty well behaved and orderly, unless someone tried to cut the line. We handled those disputes and let some family and friends in expediently as well. After the crowd was ushered into the building, I started walking toward the entry doors and the others quickly gathered behind me and we walked together. A uniformed secret service police officer was standing at each door with metal detector. When I was nearly at the door the officer standing there turned toward me, saluted me and the others and stepped aside, so that we may enter. Once inside, we saw the enthusiastic crowd listening to the local politicians that were up speaking. I saw other security personnel moving through the crowd. We then walked right up to our Chief, whom was standing on the arena floor by himself. He looked at me and simply said hello David. I responded with a hello and the others spoke to him as well. The Chief then mentioned how he could not believe that the President was here. We all nodded in agreement as we all stood there, together.

I saw a few people I had let in, so I told one of them that when the President comes out that I was going to position myself so that they could take a picture of me with him in the background. Again, the Captain reminded me that we were not to take any pictures. I then reminded him that the person that told us that could not actually order us to do or not do anything. When the time came to take the picture, the Captain jumped in on the other side of my picture, framing the President off in the distance on stage at the podium between us. As we stood there for a few more minutes, the Chief then tells us he was going backstage. That other Lieutenant, the one that had ran back to get his formal dress, proceeded to follow the Chief. The Captain then called out to him and advised him to return to post with us. He was not too happy about that, but returned he did. The rest of the detail was uneventful and eventually it all ended and we went back to headquarters and then home.

That next day, the whole upper command staff was called to a meeting in the Chief's office to debrief about the detail and to give an after incident report. Before the meeting, I had heard some rumblings about things that some people had noticed. Things that they said were not sitting well with them and these same people were white. I had not spoken to anyone, except the people I was detailed to work with but I was not feeling good about the whole detail either. The Chief started out praising us all and talking about what a good job we had done. He talked about how proud he was of us as he went on and on. Some of the other deputy chiefs and captains joined in heaping praise upon us as well.

We were seated at this big oval shaped table in the inner office. The Chief sat at the head of the table and he was flanked on both sides by; the Deputy Chiefs, Captains and then us, the Lieutenants toward the end of the table. The Sergeants and patrolman sat near us on a couple of couches and chairs near the widows in his office. I asked for permission to speak and it was granted. Then I asked for permission to stand while speaking and it was also granted. I looked directly at the Chief and began to speak.

"Sir. I can't believe that you allowed that detail to run in such a manner."

The Chief responded by asking a question.

"What do you mean?"

I quickly began to explain.

"As you know, there are only three black Lieutenants in the whole police department. So why were all of us assigned to the front of the building along with the only black Captain supervising us?"

The Chief looked puzzled, so I continued.

"Were the only people given the opportunity to see or even be seen by our first black president white cops?"

Quickly, the Chief jumped to respond.

"That was not the intent!"

"If that was not the intent Chief, then why were the only officers in formal dress on the detail white officers?"

Hearing this, a white Captain stood up and sarcastically through a question at me.

"What should we have done, if the president was white?"

I countered his question with what I felt everyone already knew.

"What we have always done, since every other president in history was white!"

That Captain quickly sat back down. Now the Chief, he started to turn red but I was not finish yet.

"Also. Why were we told that we could not enter the building during the visit?"

At that point, the Lieutenant that coordinated the action plan and that instructed us not to enter, stood up and denied.

"I didn't say that!"

A black Sergeant then stood up and said he never heard that. I looked at the black Captain that I worked the detail with and said.

"You heard it right?"

The black Captain started to stutter and was non-committal. This made me start to get angry.

"Captain? If you didn't hear that, why did you drive all the way back to police headquarters when you needed to go to the bathroom?"

The Captain just put his head down to show me his response. Disappointed, I turned away and address the Chief once more.

"Chief, I was disappointed. I feel like you could have allowed us to be a bigger part of the event itself."

The Chief dismissed us all from his office and once I was out in the hallway, a white Captain met me and shook my hand as he said.

"Those things needed to said David and I am glad that you said them."

DAVID DANIELS, III

After that meeting, I never appeared at another weekly staff meeting for the rest of my career and no one ever questioned my choice for not attending. Thanks to Lieutenant Ron Bailey, for having my back during that meeting. Although I was pissed at the department for months for the way they blatantly displayed their racism and inconsideration with the President's visit, I was then disappointed yet again to find out that I had been passed over for attending the FBI Academy. By now, I was starting to see how things would run in the department. I did not like it, but I understood what to expect and every other black officer shared my daily experiences.

How things were going on the job always affected how much I truly enjoyed having nights off. When my birthday rolled around, I was sitting at a bar watching the news as a familiar face flashed across the screen and a reporter was talking about a nationwide manhunt that was underway. The person they were searching for, whom I had known since she was a teenager happens to have been a good friend of my youngest sister. The report said that the police in North Carolina were looking for Ann Pettway. The story went on to claim that Ann had stolen a baby from a hospital in New York City, over twenty years ago and raised her in Bridgeport. Once the kidnapping had been discovered, Ann fled to North Carolina, but was now heading back toward Connecticut where she still had family. After the broadcast, I was in shock. A few people at the bar began talking about the story, but soon went back to whatever they were doing before the newsflash. I could not give it much thought at the moment, since it was my birthday and some friends joined me at the bar for a great time.

I got up early that next morning and logged onto Facebook. It was my intention to look at all of the birthday shout outs I had received from the day before and give out some thank yous. Instead, I had a message in my inbox from someone with the last name Pettway. After opening the message, it simply asked me to call the included number right away because it was urgent. I picked up my phone and placed the call. Someone quickly answered my call.

"Hello?"

"Hello, this is David Daniels. What's the emergency?"

"Okay, hold on Ann wants to speak to you."

I was not sure who they were speaking about, so I asked.

"Ann who?"

"Ann Pettway."

The voice responded quickly, but with a tone like I should have known who. Then the person handed the phone to someone else that spoke in a soft careful voice.

"Hello David, this is Ann. I'm sorry to get you into this mess, but I want to turn myself in, but I don't want to go to Bridgeport's lock up."

I paused for a minute and then told her what I would do.

"Okay Ann. Let me make some phone calls and try to make something happen."

"Alright David, thanks."

I purposely did not ask her where she was just in case things fell apart. I immediately called the Police Chief at home. I informed him of the phone call and Ann's wishes. He, in turn, put me in contact with the FBI Agent in charge of the case. In speaking with the Agent, I explained that Ann was in Connecticut and ready to turn herself in but did not want to be brought to the Bridgeport lock up. He asked me where she was and I told him about talking to her on the phone and that I was unaware of her physical location. He told me he had to talk to his superiors to get clearance for the move to a lock-up outside of Bridgeport and that he would get back to me. After hanging up, I got dressed in my referee uniform to go referee a basketball game that I had that morning.

A short time later, the Agent called back and stated that he got approval for Ann's request. I thanked him then called Ann to let her know that the deal had been struck. Then she gave me her location, I met the FBI agent and a Bridgeport Police Detective at Bridgeport's FBI headquarters. We drove to the address Ann had given me and I knocked on the door. Once the door opened, we all entered the house and there off to the left, Ann was standing calmly. I said hellos to her family members who were assembled in the same room. I hugged her and then introduced her to the FBI Agent and the Bridgeport Cop that were standing next to me. They handcuffed her and placed her under arrest. The four of us drove back to FBI headquarters. Once there, we all walked into the office building and I hugged Ann again, wished her well and then I left the building to go referee my basketball game.

The next morning before I could even get to work, the media from New York was calling and asking me for an interview and pictures. When I got to the office, the reporters with their television cameras were already there. I brushed past them and entered the building. CBS, NBC, and ABC were all trying to interview me. My friends were calling and telling me that the media was calling them also asking for my telephone number. Apparently, the news that Ann Pettway had turned herself in through me had gone global. I started getting calls from friends all over America who were watching the coverage. The New York Times and New York Post called wanting pictures and an interview and CNN also called.

I repeatedly said no to the requests, but the calls just kept on coming in while I was just trying to make it through the day. I had high school basketball games to referee in Milford after work among other things to get done. Finally, I realized the calls were not going to stop, so I relented and agreed to an interview with Good Morning America. On the drive to New Haven to do the interview, I spoke with an NPR reporter about the story. Thinking once I did that, no one else would want an interview, but I was wrong. I then spoke to News12 in Milford just before I refereed the basketball game. Once I got home that night, I knew I was done talking to reporters and spoke to no one else. I just watched the news and went to bed early.

BLACK & BLUE IN BRIDGEPORT

While I was driving to work the next morning, a friend of mine, whom I had not spoken to in the past fifteen years, was on my phone saying that they were watching me on Good Morning America. The calls kept coming in over the whole thirty-five minute drive into work. About ten or fifteen more people called and I still had to brush past some more reporters waiting outside headquarters, just to enter the building. My shift started with a debriefing of the situation by the Chief. At the conclusion, he simply said good work and that was it.

As I was leaving that day, everyone was talking to me and asking me questions about what happened. A deputy chief asked me how I knew Ann Pettway. I had one subsequent interview with the FBI and then things died down and were relatively normal again. Then the trial was set to begin and the media picked up right where they left off and started wanting more interviews with me again. Unexpectedly, a deal was ultimately struck involving Ann and there was no trial. Everything was then left to fade into oblivion. The television channel Lifetime did a made for television movie about the case and I figure they could not find an actor to play my part so it was totally ignored. In the Lifetime movie, Ann walks into a police station and turns herself into a white female officer.

Knowing that any kind of situation could jump off at any point with the job, I was always ready to help, but I also knew I had to help myself. It was clear that the department was not concerned about me or my career. So I decided to take advantage of any opportunities I could find. This led me to sign up and to attend the Police Supervisory Program at Sacred Heart University with some of my counterparts. The program was offered as an on-campus course and lasted ten to fifteen weeks with us meeting once a week until we completed the course. Dressed in department issued polo shirts, tactical pants and shorts, carrying our Apple I-Pads, we were ready to learn. Although we had guest lecturers come in, our primary instructor was a retired New York City Police Officer turned college professor. The objective of the course was to tackle different problems that were plaguing the agency and to create an overall plan to transform the department itself.

One of my classmates was a Captain that had just taken over the department's Detective Bureau. He had relationships with the Feds and other agencies. While in class on that cold December 14th of 2012, this Captain received a phone call that made him excuse himself and hurriedly leaves the premises. About a half hour later, he called someone in class to advise us the a shooting had occurred at Sandy Hook Elementary School which was just up the road twenty minutes away in Newtown, Connecticut. Fifteen minutes later, he called back and tells us that this was going to be very bad because there are mass casualties, mostly children and a few adults. First reports coming out stated there were two shooters seen leaving the school. By the time we got out of class, the incident had become global news. Twenty children and six adults had been gunned down with automatic weapons at the school by a deranged young man that had also killed his own mother before arriving at the school. The gunman ended his killing spree by taking his own life with the same automatic weapons he was carrying that day.

This shooting turned out to be the deadliest mass shooting at a grade or high school in United States' History. The police department in that town was very small. At the time, our Chief and at least two other upper level command staff lived in the town. Of course, Bridgeport's Police Department offered mutual aid and assistance to the overwhelmed town. We sent police there to assist with patrols while the officers there mourned their losses. We helped control the global media that descended on the town after the news spread. After a day or two, President Obama decided to visit the town to speak about gun violence and to personally meet with and comfort the grieving parents. Our Department sent at least twenty patrolmen and supervisors to help out with the detail.

BLACK & BLUE IN BRIDGEPORT

    Being in that caravan of Bridgeport Police cars, with our lights flashing and sirens blaring as we drove, in formation up Route 25 to Newtown to help out, is a memory that will make me proud forever. Arriving on-site, I was positioned at the school's front entry doors which were cordoned off with yellow police horses. As I glanced into the crowd, I saw a female national television news personality standing up against one of the yellow horses. Ironically, I had spoken to her on several prior occasions to this day.

    Awhile back, a Facebook friend's wife saw a picture of me on a social media site. Being a hairdresser in Connecticut, she had a few well known and some famous clients whom she did their hair on a regular basis. The hairdresser reached out to me to see if I was available. If so, she then told me that a friend of hers was interested in me. I responded with a laugh and said sure. She then told me who it was and gave me a phone number. I did call her and we spoke several times, tried to make plans to get together, but she was way too busy so nothing of substance ever developed. Now, here she was standing right in front of me with her personal assistant and at least a thousand other people looking straight down our throats. She recognized me and asked if I could get her in the building because her and her personal assistant had come up on their own to see if they could get in, but the assistant had misplaced their credentials. I walked over, moved the police horse, escorted them into the building and then into the school's auditorium. Once they were seated, she smiled at me and I turned and left to return to my post.

Chapter XI
Fighting Back
Banding Together

The Bridgeport Guardians is an organization of minority Bridgeport Police officers. It was started in the late 60's by a group of strong black officers that were tired of the racism inside the Bridgeport Police Department. They stood together with a goal of changing the conditions under which they were forced to work. Back then, the black officers were relegated to working the city's highest crime areas. When they worked with white officers, they were not allowed to drive the police cars. When it came to position, not one of them held a rank above patrolman. They could not work in any of the department's special units and they were often treated to 'nigger go home' graffiti on their lockers. The department had no shame in using 'running nigger' targets at the police pistol range and officers could be suspended and or fired at the slightest indiscretion. Black officers were belittled, disrespected, minimized and marginalized, just for being black within the police department.

As an organization, they retained legal representation and proceeded to bring litigation against the City of Bridgeport, The Board of Police Commissioners and the Police Department. Going to court, time after time, the Guardians successfully proved discrimination and its desperate impact on their hostile working environment. The victories of those lawsuits changed working conditions, hiring practices, training and promotional opportunities for all groups of minority officers and improved the system over all for individuals as well. The way the organization planned, executed and pursued the police department is known as their body of work. This body became the blueprint for other organizations across this nation changing policing in America in the process. The Bridgeport Guardians are one of the founding organizations for what was to later become The National Black Police Association, which numbers hundreds of such guardian organizations across this nation.

After winning several court case verdicts, the police department still refused to change. This led to more lawsuits and judgments against the Police Department that included the City of Bridgeport. As a result, the federal court issued a remedy order ruling. This ruling placed a Special Master over the department. This special master was to hear and remedy all the racial complaints. Since then, this process has now spanned for a thirty year period in Bridgeport.

When I was a rookie patrolman, the Guardians specifically sued the police department over the results of a recent sergeant's exam. The Guardians deemed that the test's structure was racist toward minority candidates and by design, it fit into the ongoing negative treatment of minorities by the department. In the attempt to remedy this, the Guardians then asked the courts to band scores together into groups instead of going in raw score order to try and get more of the minority officers clustered at the bottom of the list a chance to get promoted as well. The white officers that scored well on that test were against it and wanted straight score ordered promotions so the list was held up with no one getting promoted for a long period of time. This caused a lot of bad blood between blacks and white officers. At the end of the day the banding of scores was instituted and the promotions went on. On one hand, this process helped the minority officers' rise on the promotional list, but still few of them got promoted. On the other hand, it also allowed whites that scored lower than other whites a better chance at getting promoted. Over all, it left a deep racial divide within the department. Back at the police academy, one of the last organizations to address us was the Guardians' President, Ted Meekins. He did speak to us about the department's racist past and the ongoing litigation, but he also informed us of the fellowship, advocacy and community work the membership actively performed. I had been exposed to the Guardians when I was in the Upward Bound Program, back in high school and I could not wait to join. Right on the spot, I took the application filled it out and gave him a personal check of twenty-five dollars to become a member. The Guardians met the third Wednesday of every month at seven p.m. at the local V.F.W. right on Stratford Avenue. I loved going to those meetings. They gave me the chance to hear about what was going on in the department, the status of pending litigation and what was going on in the community. I also got to see the other members, be exposed to the wisdom of the elder members and get a bite to eat as well.

When I came on the job, Ted Meekins was the Guardians' President, but the organization was caught up in an internal power struggle. In 1990, Ted talked me into running for a spot on the Executive Board as a trustee and I agreed. In the next election I won that spot, but Ted Meekins lost his re-election run. The next President decided he should also hold the position of Chairman of the Executive Board. The rest of the board members felt that would be too much power for one man and that disagreement caused yet another internal riff in the organization. We fought over that for a while, but eventually decided not to let that happen. This same President then decided that he was no longer going to participate in any organizational activity. He did not come to anymore meetings or even discuss Guardian business with anyone. Not wanting to have the organization appear weak and leaderless, the board continued to meet on a regular basis and moved things forward until his two year term was up. I got really, really involved in the inner workings of the organization. This led me to go to the larger organization's meetings like the National Black Police Association's Regional and National conferences. Meeting people and learning as much as I could from other black police officers about their struggles in their police departments as well.

Toward the end of 1992, I started thinking about running for the Guardians' Presidency. I went to a trusted few officers and told them about the idea of me running. The first guy, Bobby Moss, who was a veteran officer, told me that he thought that it was a good idea and that I had his support. He also mentioned that he would run for Treasurer as well. I told another veteran officer, Ron Bailey, of my aspirations and he was dead set against it. He then tells me that I was not ready, didn't know enough yet and should wait a few years. I talked to another friend, a guy that had come on the job in the class before me and he agreed to run with me for vice president position. As word spread about it and most of the feedback being positive, I decided to run.

In November of 1992, I was elected to the position of the Bridgeport Guardians Presidency. My first four years as President were exciting and productive. I traveled to Detroit, Los Angeles, Trenton, Newark, Providence, New York, Boston, Orlando and other locales. Over my travels, I met some of the strongest and most committed black police officers spread across this nation. Meeting some, who became my best friends in law enforcement like New York State Trooper Elliott Boyce, Officer Lisa Wilson of the Buffalo, New York Police Department, Detective Shawn Kennedy of the Chicago Police Department, Carmel Precia out in the Boston Police Department, Officer James Wells of the New York Transit Authority Police, Daryl Roberts right here in Hartford, Connecticut Police Department, Sally Thomason & Kenny Ford of the Rutgers University Police Department and Massachusetts State Trooper Tanya Hicks and that is just a few. I also had the opportunity to meet the author of Eyes To My Soul, The Rise Or Decline of a Black FBI Agent by Tyrone Powers. I was also happy to meet retired Federal Marshall Matthew Fogg, whom successfully sued the Justice Department for its racist treatment while still in their employ.

With the help of my classmate, Officer Ruby Crear, we were proud to have successfully created and initiated some of the firsts for the organization. We gave the organization its first official office. To make this happen, with the help of the membership and community volunteers, we converted an old doctor's office right downtown. We started a monthly newsletter called The Guardian. We worked out a deal with a Connecticut based insurance company to provide the membership with a needed additional life insurance policy. We were proud to host the National Black Police Association's Regional Conferences that drew Officers from New York, Massachusetts, Rhode Island, New Jersey and other parts of Connecticut. We held family cookouts, joined the community in local clean-ups and even did some coaching for the kids in the basketball leagues. We did the best we could for the community and our members. We also held award banquets for the membership because most of our contributions were grossly ignored by the department. We proudly recognized minority officers for good work inside the department and the community. We also worked together and created a fair Bereavement Policy for our membership. After learning as much as I could about computers, I talked the membership into buying one for the office. Once we did, it opened up a whole new world to all of us and that led me to purchase my own.

One of the things that bothered me most about my fellow officers was that most were not very active or had much interest in these activities. I never really understood how this could be. What we were doing had so much to do with their careers and the affairs of the very communities some of them had come from. When I spoke on this bother during my travels to other locations, I would hear the same sediment expressed. In effect, if more officers were involved, it would not leave as much work for the handful that has already been so committed.

As the cost of owning a cell phone dropped, it seemed only right for me to get one. Up until this point, when daily overtime requests would be announced over the radio, we had to scurry to the nearest pay phone and call in to attempt to secure the job. When I did not make it to the pay phone fast enough, I would hear the next transmission stating no more calls please because the job has been taken. In respects to procuring overtime jobs, having a cell phone in my possession would be a quick way to beat everyone to the punch. So in the coming months, I got one and almost got fired because of it.

February 14th is Valentine's Day, but a tough day for me because that is the day my father passed. I woke up early that morning, grabbed my little Nokia cell phone and called the overtime office to ask about available work. Getting no reply, I then left the house. I tried to catch Yvette at home, to wish her a Happy Valentine's day and to tell her I would see her after I got off work. She did not answer, so I left a message on her answering machine. Leaving, I then got into my car and ran a few errands. I stopped at a store to pick up candy and flowers. I took D.A.R.E. textbooks to some of the schools locations where I was currently teaching. I stopped at the courthouse downtown and a few other places that day and finally returned home.

When Yvette arrived home, she called me and began to tell me that she had several messages from me. In these messages, she could hear me talking to people in the different places that I had been during the day. Since it was Valentine's Day, I told her to hang onto the messages, not to delete them and that I wanted to hear them when I came over. When I got to Yvette's house, I gave her the flowers and candy. She then played the messages for me. Sure enough, I could hear myself in a muffled tone talking just as she had said. All of the sudden, I felt paranoid. That feeling as if someone had been following me around all day taping my conversations. I went on to think that they chose her answering machine to deposit them on, because my number was unlisted and I did not have an answering machine. I began to perspire and worry. Although we were not living together at the time, I was worried for her and my son, David, IV. When I left that night, my mind was racing at a million miles per hour. I had been through so much already. I was not sure and wondered what to do about all this. That very next day, I contacted a black Sergeant in our internal affairs division. I explained to him what had happened and he took a recorded statement from me. I gave him all of the clothes that I had worn that day, my cell phone, my Timberland boots and Yvette's answering machine tape.

An investigation was commenced. I was told that my clothing had been sent to the FBI for forensic analysis and that an expert was in the process of running tests on my phone. They quickly asked for more information and that involved Yvette. She was interviewed and then the investigation dragged on. After about a month, I started asking questions. How were things proceeding? When could I get my things back, including my cell phone? I was told that the process would be over soon, not to worry and that the cell phone bill would be paid as long as they were using it during testing. I was reassured and just said okay. As another month was coming to an end, I started hearing rumors that I again was going to be suspended. This time around, the charge would be for filing a false report over these matters. Each proceeding week, the rumors persisted, but grew in frequency.

One day, I saw the Police Chief leaving the building. I walk over and asked him what was going on. He looked right through me and was very evasive with me. I told him about the rumors and that I thought that if things rose to his level, he would able to see that I was innocent. At that point, I decided it was time for me to take some time off and to start a plan for this new reality. I contacted the Guardians' lawyer and advised him of the case that I believed was being built against me. Our lawyer got involved and soon found out that during the investigation the OIA Sergeant decided that I had faked the calls.

BLACK & BLUE IN BRIDGEPORT

He believed that I made the calls to myself so that I could say this was part of the continued harassment connected to train station incident. From there, I could then sue the department for a million dollars. Another rumor surfaced that they supposedly paid a phone expert fifty thousand dollars to go to court and be willing to say anything that they wanted him to say.

Later is when I really found out what had happened that day. After I made a call to the outside overtime office and Yvette's house that morning, those numbers where in my recent calls. I then put the phone in my shirt pocket and as it jostled around in that pocket it made random calls. When my phone called the overtime office, someone picked up phone and after saying hello with no reply, they would hang up. When my cell phone chose Yvette's house number, the answering machine would kick in and record a few minutes, then hang up. During their investigation, they looked at my phone bill for that month because it was subpoenaed from the phone company. The bill clearly showed several calls to both locations, but they chose to ignore that fact.

A hearing was scheduled and I was advised that I would be facing charges in this matter. My attorney, back then, put in a motion for discovery to be able to look at all of their so called evidence against me. For the next few days, I sat at home and waited. My lawyer finally called me and as I answered, I could hear him laughing in the background. I said hello again and he asked if I was ready to go back to work. I repeated his words back to him, back to work? Still laughing, he told me that he had poured over all of the material and evidence that they had planned to use against me. After getting a full picture, he called the police department and told them that if they decided to move forward this case, two things would happen. Not only would he beat them, but he would also file a million dollar harassment suit against the police department and the city. Hearing this, they acquiesced and dropped all charges. In the end, they did return my things to me, including my cell phone. To no surprise, the bill was never paid. On a side note, the Sergeant that I went to in one of my darkest hours, the one I trusted because he was black like me, after interviewing Yvette, he tried to coax her into going out with him. Go figure. Sadder still, he was married at the time and I had been his DJ at his wedding.

On a Friday morning in August of 1994, I took my patrol car number eighty-three to police headquarters to get gas and to check the oil. Since it was assigned and only driven by me, I kept it meticulously clean, inside and out. While the attendant pumped the gas, I decided to clean debris from the front windshield. While doing so, I noticed a piece of white and red speckled rope hanging out from the window well where the windshield wipers sat. As I reached in and pulled it out, the rope unfurled into a hangman's noose. My heart became a lump in my throat and the hairs on the back of my neck stood up. It seemed as if the sunny blue sky went completely dark in an instant. I looked around while not believing what I had in my hand dangling right in front of me. Then I got mad! I remembered all the things I had been through up until that point and I had had enough. I took the noose straight to the Connecticut Post Newspaper. Reporter Keith Rushing interviewed me about it and all the other harassment I had faced since 1990. Their photographer, Ned Gerard, took a picture of me holding it and that was the feature story in the Sunday post that week. The department ordered Internal Affairs to investigate the incident, but nothing ever became of it. In early 1995, I filed a complaint against the City and the Police Department over this matter and won a judgment against them, yet the harassment continued.

Toward the end of my second term as Guardians President, the police department announced an upcoming Sergeant's exam and I traveled to a conference in Orlando, Florida where I heard Former NAACP leader, Ben Chavis, talking about an upcoming national event called The Million Man March. As he spoke about the event, vice president Mike Sample and I decided that we were going to attend as did many others in the room. As the date drew closer, the march was drawing a lot of negative media coverage because of its relationship to Muslim leader Louis Farrakhan. On October 13th, at Midnight, Mike and I jumped into my 1993 Chevy Blazer S-10 and departed Bridgeport, Connecticut headed to the nation's capital to become part of history at the Million Man March. Days before, I had called my cousin, who was an undercover cop in Alexandria Virginia. He agreed to put us up overnight and to come along to the march with us. Another friend, Connecticut State Trooper Ricky Meadows was coming in by train and meeting up with us as well.

We got to Alexandria about six a.m., hooked up with my cousin and went to breakfast. We ate and talked about the family then headed to his apartment. After a quick nap, we went out and picked up Rick from the train station and then just chilled for the evening. The next morning another one of my cousins along with two of his co-workers joined us. We drove to the train station to ride the train into to D.C. As we stood on the platform, we saw a sea of black men that were also catching the train to D.C. We boarded the extremely crowed train and I got the sense that something big was unfolding itself to me. As the train emerged from an underground stop, I saw hundreds and hundreds of black men. They were short, tall, fat, skinny, shabbily dressed and nicely dressed. Some were old and others were young, but all black men that were heading in the same direction toward the national mall. As we rounded the corner near The Smithsonian Institute, I saw a flurry of activity with people everywhere. The sight of all that black manhood made my heart swell with pride. It was my first and only glimpse of true black unity. People were passing us on both sides and some were selling objects as helicopters were flying overhead. Trucks from the major television stations were all lined up with reporters on camera interviewing people as photographers were snapping pictures of everything.

DAVID DANIELS, III

By nine a.m., the mall was already half full. There were large jumbo-tron screens with blearing speakers all over the place. We pretty much stayed in the area in the middle between the monuments the entire time. We did try and walk all the way up to the front at one point, but there where to many people out there for that. We brought Million Man March buttons and listened to the bevy of speakers. We saw celebrities and people that lived in Bridgeport come walking by and we took pictures with them. I looked around us. People held signs up that exclaimed where they had travelled from to get there. Being in the midst of all that brotherhood gave me a feeling I could never convey in words. I looked at Mike and he looked back at me. We raised our hands and high fived each other, smiled and spoke no words. Even with a million black men on that mall, there were no fights, arguments or any other negative behavior because we stood there in solidarity. We all took a pledge that day, the same pledge. Each one of us agreed to go back to where we had come from and to transform those communities with our own collective good works.

One of the speakers was a fourteen year old boy name Jean Baptist. I was in awe as he spoke so maturely and eloquently. I have never heard a young person with such a command of the English language in my life and he called on us all to be better fathers. When Civil Rights Icon Rosa Parks spoke, people went crazy cheering for her so loud and lasting that I couldn't even hear what she was saying. After a while, she continued her speech and with all those men out there you could literally hear a pin drop and then we started chanting Rosa, Rosa, Rosa.

Driving back to Connecticut, I felt as if my soul had been rejuvenated. With all that I had heard and seen my faith had been restored. I couldn't wait to get home and do more, much, much more. Unfortunately, when I returned to Bridgeport I was confronted with the same old demons. I still could not utilize the department radio transmission system to communicate, because offending Officers recognized my voice and were still immediately cutting me off. The quick fix was to give me a cell phone, but to do this was impractical, because there were bigger problems. The city's dispatch center equipment was probably one of the oldest systems in the state at the time. There were not enough radios in the department for every patrolman to have one. The radios had an emergency button the officers could use, but they could not identify individual radio transmitters in the field, so it was not helpful. The city was filled with dead spots where the system didn't work at all and we were recording stuff on VHS tapes.

So, I filed as complaint with the federal court. Once the case was heard, the department was slapped with almost a million dollars in fines. The Guardians' lawyer and I decided rather than strap a broke city further with that judgment, we petitioned the court to force the city to use that money to upgrade the overall system. The city quickly agreed. Grant money was also found to be included and this lead to building a combined fire and police dispatch center outfitted with the latest technology. This new system allowed each and every Officer to have an assigned radio and a charger. The new radios had their own digital signatures that were unique to them and now readable over the department software. This meant that every radio transmission could now be recorded and traced back to an individual Officer. After all of the radio harassing that was made against me and after all the court battles, finally it was the new radio system that forced that kind of vengeful treatment to stop.

In 1995, I started the Officer Friendly Basketball Camp. I remember being in Los Angeles at The National Black Police National Training Conference in the summer of 1994. I got a call from my then Supervisor Lt. Robert Kelly OIC of the community services division. He told me then that the city was giving away mini-grants to do summer programs and upon my return to Bridgeport, I drafted and submitted a proposal. My proposal was turned down. Early the next year, I submitted a refined proposal to do the same camp and got funded. My goal was to foster a better relationship with Officers and kids and to give them a safe place to be during the summer, when they were out of school. While at the camp, we provided anti-gang and anti-drug messages and quality basketball instruction at the same time. I focused on eleven to fifteen year old boys and girls. We provided breakfast and lunch and exposed them to role model guest speakers each day. I was happy to take them to the Basketball Hall of fame and later the NBA store in New York on field trips. We were also able to do family cook-outs and so much more, all at no cost to the campers.

My initial thoughts were that we would do the camp for one summer, but I was wrong. All of my children grew up in the camp as well as some of my nieces and nephews. Some of my friends in law enforcement from all over the country came and helped make it the success that it became. Police officers from New York, New Jersey, Boston, Philadelphia and Chicago pitched in to help my idea to help the children become a reality. In the end, the Officer Friendly Basketball Camp went on strong for seventeen years.

This was the early 90's and I had been out of patrol for a few months. Most white police officers in the department continued not speaking to me and some were even refusing to work with me. While the department was continually getting bad press over my daily treatment, our Chief had this bright idea to share with me. Attempting to solve two issues with one action, he came up with a plan to reacclimatize me back into patrol while introducing more officers into the housing projects. Only on an overtime basis, for a couple of days a week, two officers and I were assigned to the P.T. Barnum housing project, where I grew up. The Chief's hope was while working together, I would be able to show them that I wasn't such a bad guy and that I could be a bridge to introduce them to the residents. I agreed to the Chief's idea and was willing to do it, if they could find others to work with me. The patrol captain at the time was dead set against it. I could see the hate and disgust in his eyes as he looked at me while chomping and puffing on his cigar. No matter, he had to go along with it because it was ordered by the Chief.

The first two days on assignment went pretty well. The weather was warm and our detail started at five p.m. until about eight p.m. We walked all over the projects. Visited all twenty-one buildings and I introduced the Officers to the people I had grown up with along the way. As I introduced them to the mothers and fathers that were still living there that I still knew, we got invited into homes and even offered dinner too. We ate some of the best fried chicken in the world. On day three, all hell broke loose. As soon as we touched down in the project we started to walk toward the basketball court. This dude took a quick look at us and took off running toward building seventeen, as fast he could. One of the Officers with me recognized him as a wanted person and we all began the chase. The suspect made it to the building first and disappeared into the hallway, but an Officer was close enough to see which apartment he ran into. I got on the radio and told CAD of the occurrence. Two of us took positions on the sides of the building to prevent an escape via any of the windows. We were sent additional officers to scene and this drew attention. Now everyone who was at the basketball court, anyone that was already outside and within earshot of all the commotion came into the building's courtyard.

Within a few minutes, a Sergeant arrived and took control of the scene. More Officers arrived and the crowd was pushed back from the doorway, but we were surrounded now by all the bystanders and they are angry. The Sergeant decided to knock on the apartment door where suspect had managed to get into, but no one answered. The Sergeant proceeded to yell out that we knew he was in there and that he was going to have to break the door down. Hearing this, the crowd pressed forward and more police cars arrived on scene. We moved the crowd back a little more as a police car was brought right up to the hallway door, where we were all standing. Finally, the Sergeant and two other Officers were allowed into the apartment and after a few minutes the suspect was found hiding under a bed. He scuffled with the Officers a bit, but was quickly brought under control. Now the whole time we are there, the crowd was getting bigger and bigger and more animated. Some people started saying things like they are hurting him and we aren't going to let yawl take him out of here. I was responding to the crowd and countering all that negative conversation with all the logic I could rally up from within.

As the Sergeant and other Officers emerged from the hallway to walk out into the courtyard, the suspect was handcuffed and began to shout out into the crowd.

"They are killing me!"

To amplify his statement, he started to fall backwards as if he was hurt, which clearly was not the case. The crowd angrily pressed forward again, so I shouted out to them.

"They are not going to hurt him. Especially while I'm right here! You know me, I would not let that happen!"

The suspect was placed in a police car and whisked away to police headquarters. Trying to help the crowd disperse, I told them that they were going to end up going to jail too, if they persisted. I suggested that if they really wanted to help him to just go downtown and bail him out. After the suspect was long gone, we were ordered out of the projects and told to muster over at the local fire station, near Longfellow school. Meeting in station's parking lot, there were about eight police cars and about sixteen to twenty Officers. Our patrol car lights were still flashing, a lot of screaming, jumping up and down and Officers were high fiving and congratulating each other. One could have thought it was a super bowl victory and we were the winning team. Then out of nowhere, Sergeant A.J Perez, whom had come to the scene with the second wave of officers, yells out.

"Hey, I lost my keys out there."

Instantly, there was dead silence. After the pause, I was the only one to respond.

"Okay. Let's go back out there and get them."

The First Sergeant looked at me.

"Are you fuckin' nuts? We aren't going back out there."

I looked at A.J. I had worked with him while he was assigned to the community services division when I arrived from patrol and I spoke directly to him.

"I can get your keys back for you, but you have to go with me."

He looked back, with a worried look on his face and made his choice.

"Okay."

He told the other Sergeant that we are going back out there just me and Daniels. We took his supervisor car and drove back to the housing project. By now, the projects had pretty much calmed down and returned to normal. As soon as we got out of the car, I spotted someone I knew. I approached him and told him that while we were out here, making that arrest, my buddy here had lost his keys in the scuffle. I explained that I needed his help and that I would appreciate it if he could get those keys back. He tells me that he would help us, but then I was reassigned to another car in the area. After a couple of hours, I got a call via the police radio to return to building seventeen in P.T. Barnum at a citizens request. A.J. also heard the call and then returned to P.T. as well. We met up with the person whom we had spoken to earlier and he handed me the keys. I in turn, handed them to A.J. We thanked the guy, hugged him and he disappeared into the night. The end of day three worked its way out, but the Chief's idea of continuing the detail ended that day and we were never allowed to do it again.

A few months later, I was told a story about a call a friend of mine had taken that took him to the Mini-Stand out in P.T. Barnum. The Mini-Stand is a small variety store that was the closet store to the projects. My friend was told that a black male was at the store acting erratic. Once he arrived on the scene, he saw this kid I knew named Daryl Marrow. At the time, Daryl was drunk or high, but also upset about something that happened inside the store. A big crowd had formed in front of the store, so my friend called for backup. Just before they arrived, he had been able to calm Daryl down and was walking him out of the store.

When out of nowhere, the white arriving Officers, a male and female came busting through the crowd telling people to get the fuck out of the way. They were shoving people aside and calling them niggers as they approached. As my friend stood in amazement, the white Officers, both immediately disappeared. The crowd dragged them behind the store, kicked there asses and even took the male Officer's gun. I had worked with both of these Officers, in the same platoon, while I was in patrol. The female was always talking shit to people and was just plain nasty. While the male was one of the most racist and arrogant people I had met during my short time on the job. But I have to say, the male Officer was a changed man after that experience. He went on to take a promotional exam and made detective, because his whole demeanor totally changed for the better, for the rest of his career. The female immediately started taking sick time, after the incident and seemed to always be out injured, for rest of her career. She only lasted a few years on the job, then retired and before I retired, she passed away. Eventually, the department was able to recover the Officer's missing gun, as well.

I would love to write more about those brave men that started The Bridgeport Guardians and especially Ted Meekins but I believe that is a book best written by him, so I'm going end with these words.

Chapter XII
Needing A Boost
After Your Shift

The monetary life blood of policing, sadly to say is working overtime. The Bridgeport Police Department falls in line by being one of the lowest paid in the State of Connecticut. At this time, the scheduling pattern was four days on and three days off. Most officers could easily conclude that working overtime on our days off or any other off duty times became a must to boost our salaries. For me, it became essential while I was trying to support my children, which could not be done with my weekly paycheck. Overtime details varied in type and duties that needed to be perform. One detail could have you standing in snow up to your knees for an eight hour shift, while another have you standing in ninety degree weather in direct sunlight, for same amount of time. Officers could be patrolling a housing project trying to watch everything that is going on or sitting in a grocery store bored out of their mind. Officers could be watching actors like Martin Lawerence, 50cent or Robert Dinero make movies or you could be directing traffic away from a murder scene.

Understanding the low salary position I was in, I did all kinds of overtime details to supplement my paycheck. On one of my days off, the outside overtime office called me at home and offered me an overnight detail. For two nights in a row, someone had thrown a brick threw a grocery store window, then entered the store to steal cases of cigarettes and lottery tickets. The detail required that an officer come into the store just before it closed for the night and stay there all night to ward off another attempt at robbing the store. I took the job and showed up on time. After the store closed, I hid in the bread aisle where I could see the area where the cigarettes and lottery tickets were kept. At first, it was nice being in that aisle with the smell of bread coursing through my nose. After several hours, it became nauseating and then boring, because nothing happened the whole night. Of course, I could not wait to leave the next morning.

Another random day off, I was at home watching television when the overtime office called. This time there was a situation where the kiosk at the parking garage downtown, near the ferry terminal, had been robbed at gunpoint for the past two nights. The terminal workers were afraid and refused to work there without an officer nearby. I took the job and arrived in my own personal car, a Chevy Blazer with tinted windows. I parked right next to a pillar at the terminal. Adjacent to the kiosk, I could see into it and the street just beyond the building. I spoke to the attendant and let him know that I was there to watch out for him until he closed for the night. The first couple of hours I sat in my vehicle and tried not to fall asleep. As more time past, the attendant came and advised me that he was going to close the kiosk for a few minutes to walk up the street to Dunkin Donuts, which he did and then left.

Minutes later the attendant reappeared, reopened the kiosk. He continued collecting money, allowing entrance to the people that wanted to park there and catch the ferry to Long Island. As the night seemed to be going well, I decided to walk over to Dunkin Donuts myself and grab a coffee. I did so and then returned to my post. When I sat back in my truck, I started to drink my coffee as I was looking up the street. In the distance, there was a man walking up the street at a normal pace, nothing to be alarmed about. So I looked down to grab the donut that I had purchased with my coffee and in my mind

BLACK & BLUE IN BRIDGEPORT

I thought to myself. When I look up, the person I saw walking up the street should be at a certain distance closer. Once I popped my head up, looking where I thought he should have been, I saw no one there. I immediately turned and looked into the kiosk and I could clearly see the attendant looking directly at me with a look of terror on his face. I tilt to look directly behind him and there, I could see the man whom had been walking up the street. Now he was standing at the kiosk with a ski mask over his face as he was attempting to rob it.

I eased my way out of my truck while drawing my weapon at the same time. I slowly came around the pillar and approached the kiosk. With my weapon in hand, I told the robber to stop. Instead, he took one look at me, dashed out into the street and started running. I took off behind him pointing my gun at him as he continued back down the street towards Main Street. I yell out for the second time telling him to stop. This time he paused and then I stopped. He started to turn toward me and then he saw me get into a shooting stance. He quickly turned back away from me and started running again.

I pulled out my radio, conveyed my condition to the dispatcher, and gave my location and other necessary information, as I continue to run. He made it to Main Street first and ran across the street into a parking garage. As I cautiously entered the garage, I could see that it was open on the other side. This made me think that he had run straight through, but then I heard some noise near the ramp going up one level. Just then, one of my classmates arrived at the garage and he was a K-9 Officer. Me, with my weapon still drawn, motioned the Officer to the ramp. He exited the car, drew his weapon as he opened the rear door and his dog leapt from the back seat. As soon as his paws hit the pavement, the dog took off running up the ramp. We both followed, running right behind him. The dog ran right to a particular car and began barking incessantly. As we both arrived at the car, we could see the robber underneath. Before the dog could actually bite the robber on his head, my classmate pulled him back then the robber emerged from under the car with his hands up. I grabbed him, handcuffed him and placed him under arrest. Backup Officers found his jacket and ski mask, but no gun.

I placed him in the back of one of the patrol cars and we transported him to booking. On the way to headquarters the robber spoke out to me.

"David. Thank you for not killing me."

I took a real good look at him and recognized that he was someone I grew up with out in P.T. Barnum. He was also a janitor for the Port Authority. Later, he explained to me that he had a drug problem and was robbing the kiosk to support his habit. I wrote a report detailing the incident and forwarded a copy to the Sergeant in charge of the overtime office. That next day, when I came back to work, the Sergeant met me at my locker to thank me for a job well done. He told me that he was going to recommend me for a commendation and give me one extra hour of overtime pay. That extra hour, I did get it, but nothing ever came of that commendation.

Fifteen years later, I am a Lieutenant now. While commanding a detail of Officers, that are collecting food from shoppers at a local Stop & Shop grocery store to give to needy families during the Thanksgiving and Christmas holidays, this car pulls up and out pops the robber. As he approaches, he reaches out, shakes my hand and again thanks me for not killing him that night. The he hugs me and walks away. Later, I learned that just days before, he had completed his prison term for the attempted robbery that evening and was released.

Chapter XIII
Each One, Help One
Back Stabbing

The upcoming Sergeant's exam was formally announced with its accompanying book list outline and posted at several places thorough out the Police Department. The previous Sergeant's exam was given during my rookie year so I was not eligible to take it. Back then, I remember how it had been mired in controversy. The Guardians had not only challenged the structure of the exam itself, but also the results in court. The main complaint was that it had a negative impact on minority applicants. This impact lead to most minority exam takers getting lower scores and that put them at the bottom of the scoring list. The problem here is that this is the list used by the police department to promote officers, among other things. The Federal Court's ruling agreed with the Guardians complaint and one remedy to correct the situation was created and called banding. This was a practice of grouping exam takers scores into ranges instead of each individual being listed by their raw score. With this practice, officers could be promoted from different ranges, not just those at the top of a list. Unfortunately, this process of banding spawned more legal briefs being filed on the matter. As a result, promotions were held up and no one could be promoted off that list for almost a year. To this day, there are still bitter feelings on both sides over it.

DAVID DANIELS, III

Although the exam was structured in such a negative manner, I still promoted black officers to take it. At a Guardians meeting, I spoke to the membership about it, chiding them all to take the exam. I implored them to be serious about it and to study long and hard to insure a favorable outcome. I explained to them that at the present time, we made up forty-four percent of the department, but only eight percent of management. Some brought up the fact that at the sergeant's rank, there was very little overtime because our union contract stated that overtime hours had to be offered to patrol men first. I agreed, but reminded them how they would retire at a higher pay grade and that would be better in the long run. Also, if they had any aspirations after retirement, holding rank would look better on their resumes. Most agreed and advised me that they would study hard and take the exam.

As we moved closer to the exam date, more and more black officers were talking about the exam. So at the next regular monthly meeting, we decided to set up study groups to help anyone preparing to take it. At our first study hall, so many officers showed up we had to move it to a bigger room. We asked the two current black Sergeants to help us. One agreed to help, but only on the low. I did not understand why, but I honored his request, kept it quiet and he was helpful. The other Sergeant, a black female, also agreed to help us. She then contacted a Lieutenant Alonzo Evans, from Newark, New Jersey and he agreed to come to Bridgeport and help us as well.

When Lieutenant Evans arrived in Bridgeport, I had already put in some time studying some helpful books. There was our department's policy and procedure manual, the Connecticut Penal Code Handbook and the Motor Vehicle Law books. I read and studied them cover to cover. At the Community Services Division, where Mike Sample and I were assigned, we bounced questions off each other daily. Sergeant Judy Tesla, whom was also assigned to our division, began to help us as well by exposing us to assessment center testing. This type of testing involved role playing. There were simulated situations where we had a chance to interact with the tester as our responses were monitored and recorded in real time for later study. But as I listened to Lieutenant Evans speak about the exam, it made me realize that even though I had the knowledge, I was looking at the exam from the wrong perspective. I realized that it was my mindset that needed to change. Preparing for the exam helped me to understand that I needed to change my view from being a patrolman taking an exam to a patrolman thinking and answering questions from the perspective of a sergeant. This view is what made the difference in our studying. Patrolmen follow orders while supervisors coach, discipline, direct, and guide subordinates. Understanding this while refocusing and rechanneling our studies, made the difference. I shared this revelation with Mike and we continued to study. I wanted us to do our best. I did not want this exam to be tarnished or held up. I just wanted, all of us to collectively and individually do well. Being the leader of the group and head cheerleader, I imposed a lot of self pressure.

The exam was given at Bridgeport's Holiday Inn, which was in the center of downtown and would be administered over the course of two days. Once you entered the hotel and signed in, we could not leave the premises until we were dismissed at the end of day. Our city's civil service director facilitated the exam. It was formulated by a Dr. James Outz from Washington DC. His firm was chosen to do so, after the litigation exploded over the last exam. The exam itself consisted of; a multiple-choice potion, a role play exercise, an assessment center in basket exercise and a supervisor on scene question and answer panel. While participating with the exam, everywhere we went, we were escorted by proctors. This included going to the bathroom and we could not speak to anyone as we traveled from point to point. No beepers or cell phones were permitted and after each phase, we were escorted back to a waiting area.

During study, we were told by Lieutenant Evans to dress to impress. He told us that everything we did or said would be noted. I looked

DAVID DANIELS, III

around the room and saw a brother in a hoodie with uniform pants and army boots. I noted a white dude wearing a brown leather jacket and jeans. Remembering his words, I made sure my hair was trimmed and I was clean shaven. I wore a dark blue single breasted three-buttoned business suit. I completed it with a white oxford shirt and a red tie, which denotes power. I quietly sat in a corner of the waiting room. Off to myself, I read the Connecticut Post and USA Today, while drinking a cup of Dunkin Donuts coffee. Others in the room conversed and some looked over their study materials.

We were grouped in alphabetical order and then ushered to the first step, the multiple choice potion. I took a deep breath, said a little prayer and took my place in line. After arriving at the testing site, we were seated and given the instruction packet. We were told to begin, so I reached into the packet pulled out my test and picked up my pencil. Taking another deep breath, I dug in. I finished quickly, but just sat there looking straight ahead afterwards. I could hear papers rustling and the sound of chairs moving as people continued taking the exam. Someone sighed and then the proctor told us that time was up and to put our pencils down. Lining up again, we returned to the waiting room.

In the second testing phase, we were taken upstairs to sit in front of a panel and answer questions from our policy and procedure manual, motor vehicle law and about the Connecticut Penal Code. The testers sat there, stone faced showing no emotion, as we proceeded to answer their questions. It was hard to judge how you were doing at that time. As you spoke, they jotted notes down and checked things off on the paperwork in front of them. At the end of the session, they rose to their feet, extended their hands, shook your hand and then off you went. Back in line and going back to the waiting room. I felt pretty confident that I was doing well, but I was still a little nervous about all that was going on around me. I was glad to have this part of the testing behind me.

BLACK & BLUE IN BRIDGEPORT

Before leaving for the day, we had to sit in on our last panel where we were given scenarios that involved us in a supervisor's position on a scene. The questions centered around what you would do if you were a supervisor on a scene and certain things transpired. All our responses were recorded. Again, the panel held their stone faces as we finished this last exercise for the day. I went home, ate a small meal and prepared my clothes for the next day's testing then, hit the bed. The next morning, I rose early and showered. I chose a dark brown double breasted suit with a tan colored tie. Again, I stopped downtown to pick up the newspapers, a coffee and then headed for the Holiday Inn for the second day.

Day two was looking toward being more stressful, because of the upcoming assessment center and basket exercises. Again, I sat away from the others reading my newspapers and drinking my coffee. Around me, others were huddled together talking about the exam and bouncing questions off one another. Some people were reading study materials and others just sitting there. I made eye contact with a few people and smiled as I continued to read my newspapers. After some time, we were again lined up in alphabetical order then taken to the test site. Once there, we were seated and given the test material packets. When we were told to proceed, I opened my packet and removed the materials.

The first thing we had to do was read. The situation was that you were a newly appointed sergeant in a fictitious department. We were given an organizational chart, various department memos, letters and a calendar all relating to this department. We had to prioritize the letters and memos and take action on them based on their importance and timeliness using the calendar we had been given. We were also given a legal pad and pencil to record our answers.

I poured over all the materials within the packet, which included; a citizen had written the department a positive letter about their interaction with a patrolman, which required a written response. On the calendar, there were some scheduling conflicts that had to be discovered and then resolved. There were subordinate paperwork that needed to be overlooked for errors, corrected and action taken, if mistakes had been found. The memos needed sorting to be offered up to be read off in line-up, for the next five days or taken out of rotation. All the tasks were very detail oriented. We had to figure out what was important, what actions necessary and what corrective action needed to be taken. All of our responses needed to put on a legal pad to be discussed with another panel upstairs. After going over everything, deciding what I would do in each situation, I wrote everything down and put all my materials back in the envelope and gathered my legal pad and waited.

After some time, we were put back in line and ushered back into the room where the panel was waiting for us. I entered the room, gave them my testing number and was told to take a seat. As I sat, they began to ask what I did with each item in the testing packet. I answered their questions as best I could. Again, they held stone faces, no emotion as they jotted notes and checking off boxes on their paperwork. Then came the handshake and I am ushered out into the hallway, where the proctor is waiting to take me back downstairs. He joins me and we walk together toward the elevator and wait. Together we board the elevator, ride to the main floor and then start to walk back toward the waiting room. As we walk down the hall, someone says something and I look to see that they are pointing at me.

"Hey. You're not supposed to have that."

I look down and in my arms are my testing materials envelope and legal pad. I looked at the proctor and raised my arm out to him to give him the materials. Instead of taking them, he looks like he did not want to get blamed.

"You were supposed to give that to the panelist upstairs when you finished!"

We ran back to the elevator, back up to the testing room and handed them the materials. They apologized for not asking for the items before I left the room. All seemed well as I returned back to the waiting room to finally be dismissed for the day.

Later that same evening, while working an overtime detail that put me patrolling the Bradlees department store parking lot, I run into this butthead that had also taken the exam and he comes over to spread rumors.

"How you think the testing went?"

Before I respond, I take a look at him while I wonder what kind of response he may be looking for.

"I thought it was stressful. But either way, I feel confident that I did okay."

He agreed that he felt the same way about his performance, but then he hit me with a surprise.

"Hey. I think the testing results are going to be held up."

I had no idea what he was talking about, so I did not say a word. I guess the look on my face told him to continue.

"You know, right? Because the rumor is that some people cheated on the exam?"

I was not sure if he needed me to confirm his rumor or to just agree, but I did neither. At the time, I gave it no more thought. All I needed to do now was to get this detail done. As I continued patrolling, my thoughts were on driving out of town to attend a national black police regional conference for the weekend. After returning from the conference and getting back to work, I hear all these stories about people cheating on the sergeant's exam. There also was a petition being passed around urging the department to investigate the allegations. In the coming days, I would open up the papers to read a Connecticut Post article naming me and three other black officers as being the people that had cheated on the exam.

DAVID DANIELS, III

I was shocked and embarrassed by the time the sergeant's exam results were announced. Since taking the exam, I had been teaching the D.A.R.E. program all over Bridgeport in the schools for a while. As this news was circulating, I had no choice but to go back to each school to explain to the teachers and the students that I had in fact, not cheated at all. I spoke about that mistake I had made of not handing the materials properly. Most importantly, how I corrected it immediately and never shared what I had in my possession with anyone.

We all knew that the exam's results would not be shared with anyone for at least ninety days. At some point before then, the department commenced an investigation into these rumors. Behind the scenes, there were several officers that had been at the testing site and were in the department's day room discussing people that may have cheated on the exam and somehow my name was included. The sergeant or lieutenant on duty talked them into drafting a petition urging the department to investigate the matter. Only about fifteen people signed the complaint, which included that knucklehead that approached me at Bradlees. The petition was then drafted by another person whom could not have witnessed anything that had happened with me during the exam. We could not have been in the same places for him to see me because we were always grouped in alphabetical order. I was in the D group and he was in the Z group.

At its conclusion, the investigation had held interviews of each person accused of cheating. All of the accusers were also interviewed and the department took statements from the proctor and the panelists. After some time, the results of the investigation did yield some evidence of possible cheating had in fact occurred. Two white police officers left the testing site without being dismissed. They traveled to headquarters to pick up their checks, cashed them then returned to the testing site on that last day. A black officer had used his cell phone during the testing cycle. All of these officers were disqualified. The other officers, including myself, that were accused of cheating were fully exonerated. My complaint to the Federal Court about this treatment yielded me a judgment against the department. In the end, the signers of that petition, along with the supervisor whom initiated it all, had to sign an apology to me and received other sanctions as well. As it seems that I received some justice, at the end of the day it was not worth all that I had to go through.

When the ninety days were up, the exam scores were posted. My score placed me at the second highest overall score on the exam for this cycle of testers. Within a month, I was promoted to the rank of Sergeant. For a brief moment, things were looking up, but that quickly reverted back to the same old mistreatment. Even though there was a vacancy for a sergeant in the community services division where I was assigned, I was removed from the division and then placed back in patrol.

In early 1999, the Police Chief tried to take away my Officer Friendly's Basketball Camp. Knowing how the department and all its players always seemed to work against me, I had the foresight in the prior year to prepare to more of their dirty tricks. Instinctively, I brought the camps name and filed paperwork to trademark the camps logo as well. I never mentioned this to anyone until the day I was called into the Chief's office, where he and my Lieutenant are waiting on me. The Chief then goes on to tell me.

"Daniels, we are going to replace you as the camp's director."

Although I knew this day could come, I still felt a sense of back-stabbing as the Chief spoke. There was no clear reason that this action needed to be taken. If I did not know anything by now in my career, what would always be known is that they would never give up trying to get back at me. With a clam and clear tone, I responded to the Chief.

"I'm sorry Sir, but that can't happen. You can't replace me because I own the camp."

DAVID DANIELS, III

The Chief's reaction was typical of a man in his position expecting full compliance. He set in silence while I showed him all my certificates and paperwork. In response, his face told the story as it turned red instantly and in his frustration, he gives the paperwork to my Lieutenant to deal with. Once my Lieutenant reviewed my paperwork, he looks up to me and speaks with a defeated attitude.

"Just keep doing it, Daniels."

I laughed as I left the Chief's office to head out on patrol, but I knew they would not just let it go. Just two days later, I was given a note to again meet with the Chief. I called his office to set up another appointment, but his secretary told me he was too busy to talk to me right now. Just then, word was spreading through the department about a woman and her child being killed execution style, in an apartment on the cities north end. The B.J. Brown murder case made national news that week. In all the commotion, the Chief never bothered me again about the basketball camp. In the years to come, there would be another attempt to sabotage the camp, but I was still there to fend it off.

My first day as a Sergeant, I was nervous as hell. I had no clue as to what to expect from the patrolmen I would be supervising or the other sergeants, lieutenants, captains or deputy chiefs of patrol. But it was all settled quickly, because there was no honeymoon period. Right after line-up and as the patrol cars were making their way to their posts, a call came over the radio for a supervisor in my sector. I answered up on the radio and stated that I would be taking the call. Once on location, I met two patrolmen in a narrow hallway leading to an apartment in a two family house on the city's west side. I asked them what was going on. They advised me that they were called to this location on a call of a distraught person that had been missing and no one had seen him for several days. The neighbors feared the worst, because the person living there was a member of the armed forces, a known drinker and had weapons in the house.

BLACK & BLUE IN BRIDGEPORT

The Officers had banged on the door several times to no avail. They wanted to kick the door in to see if he was inside unconscious or worst. I quickly realized that is why I was called to the scene. They wanted me to authorize and take the responsibility of telling them to kick the door down. I asked them if the missing person had a vehicle. They said he did and it was parked in the yard. I asked one of them to check the hood to see if it was warm from someone driving it. The hood was cold so I looked around the outside of the house at the windows on the second floor. I saw that one was slightly opened in front of the house. I got on the radio and called the fire department asking them to bring a rig to our location with a ladder and basket attached to it. When they arrived, I told one of the patrolmen to get up in the basket to be lifted up to the open window. I told the other patrolmen to go back to the front door. Once hoisted up to the window, the patrolmen in the basket called out to the missing person, but received no response. He fully opened the window, entered the apartment and unlocked the door. Finally inside, we find the missing guy in the bedroom passed out drunk. He was rendered medical attention and recovered. My first day on my first call as a Sergeant was complete and off I went.

I came to love the freedom of being a supervisor, but I took my position seriously. Vowing that I would be the best sergeant the police department ever had, I promised myself. Unlike what I had experienced, I would be fair, look out for the guys under my command as best I could and I would be there for them. As a sergeant, one day a week, I had to work the booking Sergeant's desk, which I hated. This post is where people that are arrested are brought to be processed. Some are released, put in the cellblock until they post bond or transported to the city jail. The whole processing area was wired for sound and had cameras installed that were running twenty-four-seven. When my days came around, I mostly sat there and studied for the next Lieutenant's exam.

DAVID DANIELS, III

It had not been a long time that I was assigned as a Sergeant to patrol when I put in for an open position in our Computer Aided Dispatch Center (CAD). I was reassigned and worked as a supervisor of our civilian dispatchers for the next year. I liked the women and few guys that were working there. Although they were really good people, the place was like a dungeon. Situated in the basement of City Hall, we were isolated. There were no windows and that kept the area dark. The old equipment and dirty soiled carpeting did not help at all. On the upside, I was working with my boy, Mike Sample. He had also made sergeant a short time after me. Mike being there made that assignment a little more bearable.

Not long after being assigned to CAD, our Police Chief, Thomas Sweeney left the department and took a Chief's position a little further away in Glastonbury Connecticut. Replacing him as an acting Chief was my old boss from Community Services, Hector Torres. Hector had climbed the ladder all the way up to Deputy Chief by then. I cannot remember how long Hector held the acting Chief assignment, but he did not get the job permanently. Soon after, he retired and moved to South Carolina.

This was a busy period in my career and my personal life. Mike and I, with a State Trooper friend of ours, opened a fried seafood restaurant called 'Simply the best Seafood.' I started to seriously study for the Lieutenant's exam and I went back to school in the Department's Leadership Program through Tunxis Hill Community College Police Supervisory Leadership Program. I was traveling quite a bit. My most memorable trips were to New Orleans and Miami, Florida. I continued to do the Officer Friendly Basketball Camp as well. The police department did a nationwide search and test for a new permanent police chief. That process yielded a field of three finalist whom our then Mayor Joseph P. Ganim selected a NYPD veteran named Wilbur Chapman to be Bridgeport's first black Police Chief.

Chapter XIV
Who's The Leader
A New Day

Unofficially, I found out that the Mayor had an upcoming meeting with our new police chief. The Mayor had invited him to City Hall for a meeting with department heads and staff, prior to him being sworn in. As the President of the Bridgeport Guardians, I should have been invited, but I was not. I went to City Hall the day of the meeting and positioned myself where they would have to walk right by me. As they were passing, the Mayor then invites me to come along.

Once all seated in the conference room, the new Chief introduced himself to everyone. Mr. Wilbur Chapman explained to us his vision for the department and then allowed us to ask questions. When my turn to speak came around, I informed him that I was the President of the Guardians and that I knew a few NYPD officers really well. Then, I proceeded to name a few; retired Captain Eric Adams, retired Officer Ozzie Thompson who was also the former National Black Police Association Northeast regional Chairman and Officer Roger Able who also authored the book The Black Shields. Reeling off those names, I saw a twinkle in his eye and he responded by saying that he knows all of them and that I should ask them about him. Unfortunately, I had already done that and not one of them had a good thing to say about him. I never told him about that though.

DAVID DANIELS, III

During his tenure as Chief, we were treated to a show the likes I had never seen. Wilbur Chapman would be the sixth Police Chief acting or otherwise, that I had worked for up until that point. By city charter, he was supposed to live within the city limits here to hold his position, but I do not believe he ever did. He drove different luxury cars to work every day. A black Mercedes one day, then he pulled up in a white Jaguar the next. He wore a business suit and a fedora entering the department most mornings. Most disturbing was the way he spoke. He would just talk to you anyway he chose that included cursing or saying off color things. I watched him cuss a few people out along the way and all I could think was if he ever talked to me like that he was going to get it right back.

Officers never really knew where they stood with him, he ran hot and then cold. He could be cool as a cucumber one minute and totally off the wall the next. Wilbur gave you the impression that when it came to policing, he knew a little bit about everything. He introduced Compstat into our police department. Compstat was a system used in New York City as a practice of tracking and reducing crime. Reporting accurate information to supervisors in a timely manner allowed them to come up with practical responses to crime and made them personally accountable for its reduction. Without missing a beat, we started having Compstat supervisors meetings regularly. Wilbur even brought a couple of underlings with him from New York. He went almost everywhere with an entourage and could even play the vibes while he had a few department vehicles at his disposal. Shortly after his arrival and the department witnessing his character, almost every supervisor that could retire, did so. Those who remained were banished to the front desk, the dungeon that was CAD or some other netherworld location.

At this time, I was still in patrol. The Guardian's lawyer Vince Musto and I decided that we did not want to hamper Wilbur in any way with moving the department forward. So it was decided that all pending racial complaints that had been presented to the federal court with the retired Judge Robert Zampano, would be placed into mediation for the meantime. Previously, together with Chief Chapman and the City Attorney John Bohannon, we had settled several cases. I had been taken out of CAD, put into Internal Affairs to become the Internal Compliance Officer. A few months later, I was then put in charge of recruitment and reassigned again to the Community Services Division. In the middle of all this going on, I was still in school in the Supervisory Leadership Program. The department then announced the upcoming lieutenant's exam. Just like before, I encouraged our members to study for the exam, especially those who had already passed the sergeant's exam.

I loved being back in the Community Services Division for the most part, but now it was being run by a Captain whom I did not like. He was a cigar smoking know it all. Although I was being housed there, I was under the direct supervision of the Police Chief, not the Captain and I had to remind him of that fact several times. I reunited with two of my classmates; Joeann Meekins and Ruby Crear. This time around, I put together a program to recruit people from all over the U.S. to become Bridgeport Police Officers as I continued to do the Officer Friendly Basketball Camp. During this time, news was starting to emerge about Mayor Ganim being under federal investigation for corruption and that he would be going to prison soon, for the next seven years. Following that news, the new mayor John Fabrizi would step in, buy out the chief's contract and Wilbur Chapman would be gone as well. In that same timeframe, I became the President of The National Association of Black Law Enforcement Officers.

In September of that year, 9/11 occurred in New York City. This day had started out like any other normal day, if one could call our days normal back then. I got to work about eight a.m. to begin my shift. It was a sunny day, but not warm. It was more like sweater weather. I was in the office talking to my coworkers and Yvette called and asked was I watching television. I laughed and said no, she then told me to turn it on because a jet plane had crashed into one of the towers at the World Trade Center. We only had a fifteen inch black and white television in the office that would only get one channel, WTNH out of New Haven. I turned the television on and saw the tower that had been struck with smoke bellowing out of it. About three seconds passed then I see the second plane crashing into the other tower. Now my co-workers and I are looking at each other not knowing what to think.

As the second tower became engulfed in smoke, the department's phones started ringing off the hooks and activity spiked on the police radios. The television reporter was talking about what had just taken place in New York, but not one of us had any clue about what was happening. Were we being attacked by some foreign power? Were things going to start happening in Connecticut or worst, in Bridgeport? I believe an order came in for us to stand by. The next bit of news that came through informed us that it had been a terrorist attack on American soil. Additionally, there were two other aircraft that were missing and headed for parts unknown. Before we could muster at headquarters, one of the planes crashed into the ground in rural Pennsylvania and the last one into the Pentagon in Washington D.C.

New orders came in. All Officers were paired up in patrol cars and sent all over the city on patrol to keep the peace and maintain order. The next order came to cover Bridgeport's Train Station. We had to be on the lookout just in case any of the victims of the attack were going to be transported to Bridgeport because Bridgeport Hospital boasts a world class burn center. We soon got reports of people jumping from the fiery towers to escape the fire and heat. Then the unthinkable, the towers had collapsed. Many Officers wanted to jump on the train, get to New York and help out in any way that we could, but we were told that we could not.

BLACK & BLUE IN BRIDGEPORT

At some point during that evening, several news trucks came to the train station. They knew that some people working in those towers also lived in Connecticut. About eight or nine p.m., this young guy got off the train and we could tell he had been crying. His face was all red and puffy and that look, that look of horror was on his face. I would never forget it. As his family hurried to greet him, the news reporters ran toward them asking all kind of questions. He had been at work in one of the towers and was one of the lucky ones that actually made it out alive and could talk about it. We were at the train station until the last train came in at midnight. After being dismissed from this detail, I went home tired and emotionally drained, but too wired to go to sleep. After working sixteen hours straight, I stayed up most of the night watching all the news coverage of that horrible event.

The very next day at work, we were again on heightened patrol status and for the next four weeks were tasked with the responsibility of watching the city's Muslim Mosque and Jewish Synagogues just in case there was some vandalism or violence directed at those houses of worship. It was grueling as a supervisor. These details meant that I had to supervise every other day for eight hour shifts. I had not been promoted to lieutenant yet and was splitting that time with another Sergeant also assigned to Community Services to supervise the D.A.R.E. Officers. Some time passed and eventually things got back to the normal we all were left with and the results of the Lieutenants exam were announced. My scores placed me in the eleventh spot on the list for promotion. After I was promoted to Lieutenant and before he was gone, I had a falling out with Chief Chapman.

He had called me on my personal cell phone and started cussing me about some articles that appeared in the Guardian Newsletter. The current editor, Ron Bailey, who wrote under the pseudonym Rated R, criticized some of the department's brass and Chapman, himself. Thinking that I should have had more control over what was written, we argued the point loudly. I remember being ushered out of our credit union while having that cell phone conversation. Moments after I hung up, I realized that I had just cussed out the Police Chief. For the first time in a long time, I was scared to death thinking about how I was going to fired, for sure. Afterwards, Ted Meekins met with him to try and patch things up between us. A couple of days went by and I was summoned to the Chief's office. Chapman was quite cool with me as he assured me that nothing was going to happen to me because of how I responded to him on the call. He went on to tell me that he admired my passion for the job because it reminded him of him, back when he was young on the job.

The very next day, I was removed from the Community Services Division and placed back on patrol on the city's west side on a 4 p.m. to 12 a.m. shift, as the beginning of my punishment. Following that first position demotion, started an odyssey of daily events just to irritate. Each day I showed up for work, I would be told that I had been transferred to another sector. First, to the east command then to the central command and so on. As all of this was going on, I am still scared that the end of it would leave me fired. On an off duty day, I get a call from the Chief's secretary to appear in his office in full uniform the next morning. That was it! The very call that I was anticipating getting and that night, I couldn't even sleep at all. The next morning I rose early, even though it was another one of my days off. Arriving to work in full uniform and making my way to the Chief's office, I use the elevator and step off onto his floor knowing that his office is just a few steps to the right, but it all seemed like I am walking my last mile.

Finally, I enter the office and walk up the secretary's desk as she looks up at me.

"He won't have time to speak to you today, Daniels."

I simply nodded at the secretary as I quickly turn and leave the office to return back home and try to finish enjoying my days off. That next morning, I get a call from a Captain who asked if I wanted to come in on the day shift to do some paperwork. This meant some overtime for me, so I agreed to come in the next morning at 7:30 a.m. That morning, as I am standing behind the building on the back deck, near the gas pump and stretching, I see the Chief as he is arriving at work. I speak out to him saying hello, but he looked right through me as he rushed into the building. About two minutes later, the Captain comes running outside looking beet red and sweating, saying he needed to talk to me. I followed him back into the building and he begged me to go home, right now. I asked him why and he explained that the Chief had called downstairs to ask him what I was doing in the building. The Captain, being too afraid to tell him that he had hired me to work overtime, decided to ask me to leave instead. I tell the Captain that I would leave, but only if he gave me twenty hours of comp time on my books. I expected a little resistance from the Captain, but I understood that the fear of the Chief was more important to him, so he quickly agreed and put the time on my books. I smiled and went back home.

Paranoid for weeks, I kept wondering and trying to figure out what the Chief was going to do to me next. Meanwhile, our mayor was in the midst of a political corruption trial that was being sensationalized by heavy news coverage. In the end, he was convicted and had to leave office. Common Council President, John Fabrizi then took over as mayor to finish Ganim's term. Him and the Chief Chapman, did not get along at all. The rank and file seemed to love Fabrizi, as I noticed overtime became plentiful for everybody, except me. Although the new mayor brought out the Chief's contract, some of the people in patrol knew that I was in his doghouse so I was overlooked for overtime.

Then a wonderful day came when I arrived to work to find the shift Sergeant smiling in glee at me. I quickly wondered what was going on that was making him this happy. The expression on my face must have silently asked the question and he could not wait to tell me.

"Go upstairs."

Expecting the Sergeant to blurt out some new news or some other development left me unprepared for his direction and it showed in my response.

"Why?"

"It's okay. Just go up there and tell me what you see?"

Curious, I agreed and then jumped on the elevator. Once upstairs, I went into the Chief's office and looked around in amazement. All of his pictures and personal things were gone. I ran back downstairs and the Sergeant took me out to the police garage. He then directs me to look into one of the department's SUVs parked nearby. I peeked inside and saw all of the Chief's things that were missing from his office. I turned and looked at the Sergeant, this time with a matching smile on my face as he shares the good news.

"We are waiting for someone from city hall to come over with a check. Then, we can transport the check and all his personal effects back to him in New York."

I had no words to respond to the Sergeant, but he could tell that I was overwhelmed. Without another word, the Sergeant turns and walks back into the building. Just like that, Chapman was gone! I immediately dropped to my knees.

"Thank you, Lord!"

Enter Deputy Chief Anthony Armeno. He was to serve as acting Chief until the Civil Service Division could put together a national search to hire someone permanently. Within a few days, the acting Chief placed me back into the Community Services Division, returned my take home car and even issued me a company cell phone. Things were looking a whole lot better in just a few days.

The Lieutenant in charge of the Division decided that he wanted out, so he returned to patrol and I was made the Commander of the Community Services Division. My crew and I continued to teach crime prevention and do workshops for the community. We taught the D.A.R.E program, the Officer Friendly Basketball Camp and we organized food and toy giveaways during the Easter, Thanksgiving and Christmas holidays.

Life was pretty good. We were doing good works and getting a hefty chuck of departmental overtime. We hoped that Armeno would get the Chief's job permanently, but his past troubles started to pop up. He had gotten into some trouble years ago with another officer and people started bringing up that situation while protesting his possible appointment. This promoted the national search for a new Chief and Mayor Fabrizi then selected former New Haven Police Supervisor, Brien Norwood to become the city's next police chief. I had known Norwood since he was a little kid. His father, Mr. Alexander Norwood was my fourth grade teacher and one of my biggest role models. To avoid a long drawn out story, my role models' son was nothing like is father.

Mayor Fabrizi finished Ganim's term and then got elected in his own right. I loved him as Mayor. If Fabrizi wanted to talk to you or needed you to do something, he would call you direct or invite you to his office at City Hall to talk. He was very personable and down to earth. He also appointed me as the liaison between the schools and the police department. Unfortunately, after his first term in office, Fabrizi let personal demons and a bad decision ruin his chances of getting reelected.

Enter the Bill Finch Administration, which I thought held a lot of promise. I had met Finch at a Black-Tie fundraiser that was sponsored by Former NBA Basketball Player, Charles D. Smith. Only having a few years on the job, Finch and I were seated at the same table. When I went to introduce myself to him, he told me that he knew who I was. Finch went on to say that knew my history in the department and how I had been treated by my fellow officers was wrong. What I did not know at the time he became Mayor is that he would be bringing some of the most evil people to Bridgeport to work with him. What I learned after her arrived is that they would be treating me far worse than any of my fellow officers did.

Chief Norwood was young and aloof. Not engaging at all and more like a kid in many ways. He wanted the officers to have all of the toys; new cars, tasers, segways, etc. New cameras were installed in and on the building. Norwood had our headquarters painted and the parking lot paved, while adding new security fencing around the perimeter. He changed the style of our badge, gave us challenge coins, and even took us to visit his buddy that was running the Providence Police Department. All of it was tantamount to putting new paint on an old rusted car.

After all that Norwood had changed, he then attempted to change the attitude of the supervisory staff of our racist institution. He had no idea what he was up against and made the mistake of not finding out, before he tried. Norwood would not listen to any black officers in the department, including myself. It was rumored that while he was pushing for change, someone broke into his house, urinated in his refrigerator and left human excrement on his front lawn. He had also mentioned that people had gone thru his trash. While under Norwood's command, Sergeant Joeann Meekins came to work one morning to find a hangman's noose sticking out from one of our patrol cars.

At another point, he decided to transfer a few officers out of my division and advised me that everyone remaining would be assigned to a school. I had one officer working with senior citizens at the time. She did not want to be reassigned to a school so she started a campaign to keep that from happening. She had the seniors marching on her behalf and people lobbying to keep her out. Norwood simply ordered me to put her in a school anyway. I assigned her to a school near our office, trying to follow orders and trying to keep her close. The Officer then filed a lawsuit against us both, alleging discrimination because of her age, gender and race. I could not believe it, but shortly after those charges were brought, Norwood started secretly looking for another job. He was not forthcoming about his job search until he secured a position. It hit the news first and then it was planned for him to be off to Richmond Virginia to become their Police Chief. The night of his little going away party, someone in the police department had his car towed as a parting gift. Ultimately, Norwood was dropped from the lawsuit, but I still had to deal with it. Intuitively, I had been collecting information on that Officer's coming and goings. Documenting some things that she had been involved with that weren't quite right. I passed that information on to the city's attorney and the litigation was withdrawn.

Mayor Finch decided to fill Norwood's absence by appointing my old boss, Deputy Chief Joseph Gaudett to the acting Chief position. Finch's administration was very hands on when it came to dealing with the police department. At some point, they decided that Chief Gaudett was going to be their choice for the next Police Chief. Leaving him in an acting capacity long enough for him to get his bachelor's degree, they went through the motions of a national search and test, but immediately picked him as the new chief. The administration strung him along for awhile then granted him a five year contract. From the very beginning of Gaudett taking the position, anyone could see that things were going to be very different.

Almost from step one, we all could see who was running things. Chief Gaudett did not even try to hide it. In our Compstat meetings, the Chief would out right say that this is what the Mayor wanted. This is what stopped me from attending future meetings. Surviving Gaudett's leadership was like being on a rudderless ship. We were going in all sorts of directions, things no longer had rhyme or reason and people just did whatever they chose to do. Officers formed these little factions within the department, carving out fiefdoms and insolating themselves from the evil that now lived in city hall. Over the course of my career, I had been praised for my work and now, all the sudden, things started going south. At first, it was small stuff like falsely accusing me of using the company's email system for personal things. Then it became complaints about misspelling words or using slang on our Facebook and Twitter pages that I created and managed. These complaints were directly about me and I got fed straight to the loins, without a buffer. Around this time, I was coming into my twenty-fourth year on the job which meant I would be eligible to retire in just a year.

As I began to raise my voice more often about things inside and outside the department, the more attention I received from what I started calling, the evil empire. I and a few other friends started working with this group called Connecticut Against Violence in 2012. Our attempt was to try and meld law enforcement and the hip-hop culture to stop all the shootings and killing of young people in our city. Very quickly we were able to do some good things like; talk to groups of teens, provide music at high school basketball games and take kids out of the city on field trips. As we began to garner a lot of positive press, the evil ones did not approve. I remember being called to the Chief's office several times just to explain what we were doing. It was made clear to me that I had to tell the Chief everything that was being done, which I did not mind, because he was the boss. Days later, that instruction was extended to the Mayor's press secretary. Now this instruction, I did reject for meaningful reasons. No other police officer that I knew of had to meet this demand and most of what I was doing was on my own time.

On another occasion when I had to go to the evil empire and meet with them, I was directly told that I was not complying with their wishes. In a short response, I expressed that I had no intention of doing so either way. So that meeting was a short one and I was dismissed. My reaction was well within the normal course of business for the police department. As an officer, I was obligated to only report up and down the chain of command in the department and that did not include the Mayor's press secretary. As I was leaving, I saw the Chief Gaudett walking into the building to meet with them. Seeing him made me quickly realized that I would be in trouble. Although technically, I had done nothing wrong, I knew there would be trouble. By know I had a good idea what could come from this situation. If worse came to shove, all they could do was transfer me out of Community Services again or place me on midnight shift until the end of the year.

A short time later, just as I expected, I started hearing the rumors that I was going to be transferred back to patrol and placed on midnights. Near the fourth of July, I was told by the only black captain in the department that the deal had been struck and I would be getting transferred back to patrol by week's end. The very next day, I saw the Mayor at a community meeting and asked him about the transfer. Finch played ignorant of the information, but went on to say that the Chief had some tough choices to make. Later that day, I made a call to the Chief and was told that he thought a change was necessary. I simply replied with an okay, but quickly asked that I be allowed to do the Officer Friendly Basketball Camp before beginning the transfer. The Chief agreed to my request and then I did the basketball camp. Somehow, the media got wind of the upcoming transfer and started asking questions. A community rally was put together for people to gather on City Hall's steps. About twenty people from the community came out in support of me not being transferred. A news reporter onsite, who had followed the success of the basketball camp and had previously interviewed me on camera, seemed disturbed and had something to say to me afterwards in private.

"I've watched you over the years helping thousands of people. Maybe even enough people to fill the baseball stadium, but I don't get it. Not even enough people came out for you today to even fill the sidewalk?"

The reporter displayed confusion all over his face and disappointment in his voice and I understood what he meant.

Although I was hoping for more support, I always had a higher focus and I hoped he could understand.

"The things that I have done over all these years, I did for love. I appreciated all the opportunities I have had to be there, when I was needed. I have no regrets for any of it. But what hurts me is knowing how sad things can get around the holidays for so many and I won't be there."

Shortly after the community rally, I was transferred to midnights and back into patrol.

On my first day back into patrol in 2012 I started retiring from the department. Although I would not officially retire until April 12, 2014, I never performed to my usual high standards another day in that police department. I went to those midnight shifts until January of 2013 knowing I was just a bump on a log. I was assigned to patrol in the Central Command which covers the downtown area up to the city's north end. My duty was to be the Sector Supervisor over the Sergeants and Patrolmen working the sector as well. Then my seniority kicked in and brought me back to day shifts. I quickly used all my sick days, personal days and three weeks of my vacation days, just to be away from the job. As for my passion, I held the Basketball Camp one last time on my own time without the city's backing. My remaining two weeks of vacation were spent, at a gym that was not a part of the school system, with the children in the camp. In the end, I was proud of the seventeen years that I had the privilege of serving Bridgeport's kids. I had knee replacement surgery that October and stayed out for five months recovering. Returning to work in April of 2014 for just five lonely days and then I officially retired.

Chapter XV
Farewell Tour
Next Episode

Having been so inactive while stuck at home during my recovery from knee replacement surgery, I actually continued not to do much that first month of retirement. I exercised, watched television and tried to get better and stronger. After a few weeks, I was able to get around a little easier and finally able to drive again. I went to physical therapy and ran small errands for myself, but nothing to strenuous. As I sat around and watched as my new beard grew in, I began plotting my new future. My conclusion, it was about time that I start seriously considering running for mayor.

Being home that whole winter was nice. I did not have to deal with the snow much at all because my neighbors kept my driveway shoveled and cleared. My real friends brought me food and supplies, when I needed them and checked on me from time to time to make sure I was alright. By the spring time, I was walking really well and ready to go back to work. I saw my Doctor at the end of March and he released me to go back to work full duty.

I then took my medical release papers to police headquarters to advise them that I was fit for duty and could return to work. A few days passed and I heard nothing from anyone. I called the Chief's office to see when I would be able to return to work. I was told someone would be getting back to me, so I waited. A day later, I got a call from one of our Deputy Chiefs. I asked him when I should return to work and he replied by asking if I planned to retire come this June. A bit puzzled by his question, I replied with a yes, because that was my intention. He then told me that he would call me back and give me a date.

My expectation was to return to work and my position on the day shift. What I did not know was that there had been a Lieutenant working days in my position and he had taken a temporary job assignment with the condition that at its end he would be allowed to return to the day shift. Learning this, I understood that they had already permanently replaced me. Although I outranked the Lieutenant in question, that assignment was now coming to an end and he expected to come back to work my position. Had I not told the deputy Chief that I was going to retire, I may have never made it back to my position. In fact, they were going to stick me on either the 4 p.m. to midnight or midnight to 8 a.m. shift that were generally filled by lower ranked officers.

At the time, I was the second highest ranking Lieutenant in the department. The Deputy Chief called me back and told me to start Monday April 8, 2014. I returned to work and told myself to try and think of any good reasons why I should stay. I gave myself until lunchtime to come up with some good reasons. Unfortunately, I could not think of one good enough to stay. After my shift was over, I walked over to City Hall and walked into our benefits office. There I happily signed the papers to officially retire in five days which would be Saturday April 12, 2014. Those next few days were my farewell tour. I tried to see everyone that I liked within the department to say a proper good bye. I visited businesses and stores in the city letting people know that at the end of the week, I would be retiring.

Friday April 11th came quickly. I arrived at work at about 6:15 am and started my work day. I addressed both morning line-ups advising the patrolman and sergeants in attendance that it was my last day at work. I told them that it had been a pleasure working with them and I wished them all well, dismissed them, shook a few hands and hugged a few people. I went out and got into my squad car for the last time and headed downtown. I stopped at Dunkin Donuts and took a farewell selfie with the crew working behind the counter. A couple of my friends, Lew Rock and DJ Tony Crush came through and we all got coffee and took a few more selfies.

I left downtown and headed toward the Stratford Avenue Area to say good bye to the people in that area. I rode around the sector for a few hours then headed back downtown and took selfies with other people that I came across. I posted all the pictures on Facebook, then the congratulations messages started popping up. At lunchtime, I drove over to the hollow and had lunch at The Red Rooster Restaurant. After finishing my meal, I took another picture with the owner and his daughter then back on patrol.

About 1:30 p.m. I went back to headquarters to use the bathroom. I ran into one of the Deputy Chiefs. He looked at me a little sideways, but then smiled.

"You still here? On your last day? You know you can leave, if you want to?"

I shook his hand and happily responded.

"Thank you."

Heading out to my personal car, I retrieved an empty box I had placed in the trunk. First, I emptied my locker and then headed upstairs to turn in my department issued equipment. I paused at the elevator to use my department's radio. Saying one final good bye over the airways to the units in the field and our dispatchers, I then pressed on and went upstairs. I turned in my weapon, the magazines, my department radio and the IPad that I used for school. From there, I went to the Chief's office to shake his hand and wish him well. I walked across the hall to the Assistant Chief's office and did the same then left the building.

DAVID DANIELS, III

Walking toward my car, I paused. Turning around, I looked back at the building, smiled and then went home.

Sitting at home, the thoughts of running for Mayor were still in the back of my mind. A call came in from a guy that I had met on a trip to Dallas, Texas a few years prior. I had done some work for him by helping him sell a cellphone app that he had created, to assist the community in reporting crime for law enforcement, now he was offering me another job. This job included traveling, a six figure salary, stocks in the company and other perks. A few conference calls later, a trip to North Carolina was planned and I arrived to partner up with a team he had assembled to do a presentation. We were then told that on a subsequent flight to Dallas, Texas we would be offered contracts to officially start working for him. Once in Dallas, the team worked for four days on a presentation that was presented to the Dallas Police Department. That presentation went well, so we were told more about the company and our future positions in it. On the last work day, the team was given a test on a part of the system that we needed to know, but were not presented with any contracts. Back on the plane and back to Connecticut I went.

For the next week, I heard nothing about the job. Another member from the team started calling me and asking me if I had heard anything from Texas. I advised them that I had not. I started making calls, leaving messages and nothing, no returned calls or any contact. Next, a team member sent me an email package that he had received from Texas advising him that no more progress toward employment could be gained at the moment. The information stated that until some additional skills like mastering Microsoft Office and some salesmen skills were mastered, no hiring could be done. I called Texas and received the same information email packet, but I also learned some more news. The company tells me that both of the group's presentations won the company their bids that they were seeking. But now, all of these skills that they were asking about, that a normal person could acquire over time, they wanted us to learn in just weeks or no job offer. Sadly to say, we were never compensated for that work we did in North Carolina or Texas, that was good enough to land the company new contracts, but not good enough to land us jobs and that was the end of that.

This woman that I was vaguely familiar with started calling me to tell me that I should strongly consider running for Mayor. Her weekly calls became daily calls, but even though I wanted to run I was not quite sure that I should. Finally, we agreed to meet and she again continued her pitch.

"You have a lot of support out here David. You should strongly consider doing it."

We met a few more times when she proposed posting a Facebook page asking the question: Should David Daniels III run for Mayor of The City of Bridgeport? That first night it went live, not only did the question get six hundred likes, there were several positive comments and even pledges of support. I could not believe it. I called a guy that was very astute at assessing the city of Bridgeport's political arena and he agreed that I had a chance. He pointed out that people knew and liked me, so if I could raise enough money I would have an outside chance. He also told me that the incumbent Mayor had made a lot of enemies and that people were looking for a change. He asked if I was going to run as a democrat or independent candidate. I told him I thought I might have a better shot as an independent, he agreed. He also mentioned that if I tried to get the democratic town committee endorsement it would be harder and even more expensive to compete. Shortly after our chat, the rumors came rushing in.

Rumors about the recently released, convicted former Mayor Joe Ganim was now testing the waters for a possible run as well. In the coming weeks, the lady that I had been speaking with set up a couple of community forums for me to speak to the people. We did several forums on Saturdays at the Bridgeport Public Library downtown. We only drew small crowds, but it was enough to sharpen my skills as a perspective candidate. In those forums I learned the citizens' concerns and how to speak to them. Soon the media started calling and asking me about my intent. Since I hadn't committed to actually running yet, I told them I was still thinking about it. Then I started to hear the negative comments people were making; like the fact that I had lived out of city for a while and that would be an issue with them. Some said the fact that I did not own any property within city limits meant I was not currently paying taxes into the city was an issue for them. I just plowed ahead learning as much as I could along the way. I started reaching out to people I thought might be willing to help me.

I have to admit here that almost of the people that I expected to help me, including close personal friends, did not. The people that I never thought would help me, helped. As I would come to learn, the people I had no previous relationship with would become my biggest supporters. One of my greatest disappointments was watching one of cousins, not only side with, but become my opposition's biggest cheerleader. On the other hand, my big sister told me she would help and she stood with me all the way to the finish line. Always loving you Deb!

I was featured in a few articles and fodder on a few blogs. I hooked up with a group of guys also considering running for elected office as well. All of them had ran in a race or had been elected to political office before, they taught me a lot. We met weekly and discussed issues germane to what we were trying to do. We also did a few collective community forums around the city. Again, that was good experience to get in front of a crowd to talk about issues and interact with other people in the arena. We decided to stay together and continually meet up to see who would emerge as the strongest candidate with the agreement that whoever that would be, the rest would back him.

After all the talking and meeting up, one guy opted to try and win an open state representative seat, but lost that race. Another guy decided he did not want to continue running, so he joined Gamin's camp. Those of us that were left decided to run on our own. Two sought the endorsement of the Democratic Town Committee and lost when the committee endorsed the incumbent mayor. When all the smoke cleared, the incumbent Mayor lost the primary bid to the former mayor and now we had those two, plus the five of us running for the executive position.

I was not eligible to participate in some of the debates because of various rules set forth by the entities that sponsored them, but I attended them all. For all the other debates, I played an active part which included television and radio coverage. I was finding it very hard to raise money. People that I knew and thought would be supportive, so that I could win and be the kind of mayor they deserved, did not donate much. Maybe it was because they did not think I could win or maybe they just did not have the money to spare. Who knows? Either way, some of the situations I have experienced with my own people, were the most disappointing and unforgettable. Only to be outdone by those who blatantly showed no support, while rubbing it in my face and loudly proclaiming that they were supporting my opponent.

There was a prominent black business man who was doing business in the city. He had bugged me for months just prodding me to run. Every time I ran into him, all he wanted to talk about was me running. Trying to entice me, he once expressed that when I decided to run that he would give my campaign a ten thousand dollar check just to get me started. When I finally decided to run, I called him to advise him of my decision. Without hesitation, he asked me to meet him at a local bar and restaurant downtown, so I go. We meet up and he handed me a sealed envelope and told me that he wished me luck. I shook his hand, thanked him and did not open the envelope until I got home. As I took a seat, I pulled out the check and realized it was written for one hundred and fifty dollars. I am not sure if things had changed for him or was he sending me a signal that he no longer believed in me. I had no idea. But he could have given me a heads up, because when I saw that check, I almost fell off my chair.

Another black business man called me to come to his office, so I went. As soon as I sat down he told me that I was going to lose. He continues by saying that he was voting for and working with the opposition as he handed me a check for five hundred dollars. I quickly asked why he thought I was going to lose, if he was really supporting someone I was running against and why donate to my campaign? He replies by saying that at the end of the day, he did not want his name to be on the list of blacks in this city that did not help me. It was an eye opener, but I understood his reasoning. I thanked him for his honesty, his donation and shook his hand as I smiled and then left.

I was hosting a fundraiser at a local restaurant when the owner's brother came out of the kitchen, saw me there and took that opportunity to begin bragging about giving the opposition a five hundred dollar donation. He then came over to me, shook my hand then proceeded to walk out of the business. As he walked away, I could not help but to think. Was I suppose to smile in his face, show a lack of support for him and walk off in all the times he had come to me with parking tickets over the years?

I just couldn't understand those that I thought were my people. I opened up the paper one day to see a picture of a woman holding a drink in her hand at the opposition's fundraiser. She was proudly talking about him being her choice and I couldn't help but think back on a time when I appeared at her door during the Christmas holiday with toys for her daughter when I knew she was dead broke and getting electricity from the apartment next door.

Over all and pushing donations aside, I had hoped that those, whom I appreciated the chance to be able to help over the years and had good feelings about, would have been more supportive of my run. Considering that everyone is entitled to pick and support the candidate they choose, I still wished that some would have considered not blasting their non-support in my face. Unshaken, I pressed on with the little money I had and the wonderful all-volunteer staff that successfully helped me to secure a spot on the ballot as one of the seven candidates.

On Election Day, at a school near my hood, I had to walk past people that; I grew up with, that I had personally looked out for, that I had worked to keep them out of jail at some point and even some of their family members. They were all out there working and supporting my opponents. Seeing this was confusing and honestly, made me sick to my stomach. I moved on and went to visit another school up on the north end. After parking, I got out of my truck and walked toward a friend that was volunteering for me that day and was in a heated discussion with a few men. As I approached, someone looked up and saw me, and then they all went silent. I greeted everyone there and then a seasoned elected official looked at me and had something to say.

"After all this is over today we need to sit down and talk. I don't like the division I'm seeing here today."

Without breaking my stare at him, I quickly responded.

"Now that's a conversation we should have had before Election Day, don't you think?"

He agreed, but then I looked down at his hands to see that he was passing out handbills supporting one of my opponents. He was there to urge the people venturing into the school to vote for that person. After seeing this, I had more questions.

"Why aren't you supporting me?"

"Because my candidate is an old friend."

He seemed sincere about his connection to his candidate.

"Well, how long have you known her?"

"For eight years."

I was a little disappointed with his response because I could not understand his logic, so I probed him.

"Well, how long have you known me, my mother and my father?"

DAVID DANIELS, III

Without a pause, he seemed to be proud to answer the question as if he could not understand why I even asked.

"Since you were a little kid!"

I smiled inside as I leaned into him and said my final statement.

"And now, I'm over sixty years old."

Before he could even think of a comeback, all of the men standing there gave him that slanted head, wide eyed look that quietly asked: what you going to say about that? Not another word was said as we all turned and walked off leaving him standing in that very spot. What I was having issue with is a feeling that my people were just giving away their support. Seemingly, without thought or hesitation to those whom we all knew would not work in their best interests. This man, a smart man, an elected official who was supporting an opponent because that opponent is an old friend of eight years did not see any conflict in not supporting a sixty year old family friend. It saddened me. But making me feel worse was the fact that he actually worked with my father at Carpenter Steel, back in the day. These kinds of situations reminded me of something a prominent Latina politico insider had told me back when I filed my papers to enter the race.

"David, you're a good guy, so I'm gonna share this with you. See all of these people that are cheering you on this morning? Well the truth is most of them are going to turn their backs on you this afternoon."

Truth be told, she was only off by a couple of hours, but I soldiered on and learned a lot during the process and about the process. In the end, I would be still waiting on some people to return my call of support two years later, go figure.

Former Mayor Joseph Ganim won in a landslide victory. I received only five hundred four votes. Although my biggest disappointment wasn't losing to Ganim, it was more heart shattering to witness black people, my people not displaying enough unity to take control of their own destiny in a city, our city that is mostly comprised of minorities. Instead of demanding more from their government or taking a chance on electing one of their own, they settled with accepting more of the little to nothing that they had been getting. It was sad to see how easily they continue to support a corrupt political system that has marginalized, disenfranchised and locked them out continuously for decades. To the point of caring so less of them, it blatantly only offers plans to continue doing the same into perpetuity, because they know they have their repeated vote.

A few days ago, I turned sixty-four years old. I never thought I would make it this far. At times, it seems the deck was stacked against me. I was and am a fighter, so I fought and clawed my way through. Just as Dr. Bellows had predicted, during my rookie year I was injured in three car accidents, sued, investigated by internal affairs, brought up on charges, suspended and divorced. Unfortunately, he could not have warned of the slew of internal dangers that rained down on me, but I wish he could have.

To this day, there are officers that still refuse to speak to me or acknowledge my presence. This is the result of my choice to honor my oath to serve, to the letter, when it mattered most. I am not perfect, but I did what was right and what had to be done, unknowingly at the cost of derailing my career. As tough as it got, I made it a point to continue showing and being a good example every single time I put on that uniform. That standard was my standard. I did it, not just for me and other adults, but always for the children. Through all the dark times, my strength to continue came from teaching D.A.R.E., starting the Officer Friendly Basketball Camp, serving as one of the Presidents of The Bridgeport Guardians and being there for those whom I knew needed an officer to be there for them. Just like Officer Lafayette White. Who, many years ago, showed a group of children growing up in the projects that an officer, just like me, can be a positive role model, if he or she so choose. With this, I could not see doing it any other way. Sadly, the seeds of racism planted so many years ago within our police department are not just still present, but are being allowed to grow and fester, without restraint.

I had been a Bridgeport Police Officer for twenty-five plus years now. I had had many experiences, good and bad. A lot of my career was played out in the media and most people know about; The Bridgeport Guardians or National Black Police Regional Presidencies. My attaining the rank of Lieutenant, The Officer Friendly Basketball Camp, IWatch, The Million Dollar Youth Build Grant, The Thanksgiving and Christmas food and toy programs, The DARE and GREAT Programs I taught, like The Ann Pettway Surrender, etc, etc. If anyone was around to hear someone ask about my most fulfilling memories, I wouldn't have been talking about any of that.

Throughout my career, the things I was able to do that made a difference in the lives of Bridgeport's children are my fondest memories and those are the things I would be discussing. I have consoled and counseled thousands of Bridgeport kids and the good Lord put me in places to help them even when I didn't know that was going to be the plan. One evening I was invited to Longfellow School to a Father and Daughter dance, so I went. As the evening wore on and the fathers were socializing with their daughters and having a good time, there came a point in the evening when the DJ played a special song. This song was played so that all of the father's could take their little girls on the floor to partake in this special dance. As the music started to play, I honed in on a little girl standing on the sidelines. I could tell she wanted to be on the floor with her classmates, but she was accompanied by her mother, as her father was unavailable to attend. I reached out my hand to her and in full police uniform took her out to the middle of the floor and danced with her like her father would have. After that dance she was like the bell of the ball. And for the rest of the night, that smile never left her face.

In this career there were many times when the gun and badge were tucked away into the closet. But it's the memories of times like the

BLACK & BLUE IN BRIDGEPORT

Father and Daughter's dance that still make me smile and be proud to have served on the force and been Black and Blue in Bridgeport.

ABOUT THE AUTHOR

BORN IN BRIDGEPORT, Connecticut the second child of six children, David was raised in The P.T. Barnum Housing Project, educated in Bridgeport's public schooling system and attended Norfolk State University.

After working for Southern New England Telephone Company for several years, he joined The Bridgeport Police Department in 1989. During his twenty-five years of service, David proudly served in various positions and divisions such as: Recruiting, Communications, Internal Affairs and Community Services. Additionally, his joy came from participating in yearly Thanksgiving and Christmas food and toy giveaways to needy families, teaching the D.A.R.E. and G.R.E.A.T. programs in Bridgeport Schools and creating The Officer Friendly Drug Free Basketball Camp, which all served thousands of Bridgeport Boys and Girls during their years in operation.

David would finally retire as a Lieutenant in 2014 while serving in the Patrol Division, but left the department holding several local, regional and national awards. To include: The State of Connecticut's Legacy Citation and the NABLEO President's award. Mr. Daniels has also served as the President of the Bridgeport Guardians for five terms, the Vice President of the National Black Police Association North Eastern Region and then the first President of what became N.A.B.L.E.O., The National Association of Black Law Enforcement Officers. Formerly he has been a presenter for the National Basketball Association's Rookie Transition Program, the owner of a local restaurant 'Simply the Best Seafood' and an on air disc jockey for WYBC Radio.

During his retirement, David Daniels, III continues to speak publicly advocating on behalf of the people of Bridgeport and is available for consultant work for those who need him. Privately, he continues to improve his culinary skills by indulging his passion to bake as he patiently awaits some grandchildren to spoil.

DAVID DANIELS III
P.O. Box 5355, Bridgeport, CT 06610-0355
Daviddanielsiii@hotmail.com
Follow me on Twitter: twitter.com/david31956
Subscribe to my blog: david31956.wordpress.com

To the Newtons

Thank you for the love and support